T0184130

Lecture Notes in Artificial Intelligence   12316

Subseries of Lecture Notes in Computer Science

More information about this subseries at http://www.springer.com/series/1244

Samarth Swarup · Bastin Tony Roy Savarimuthu (Eds.)

Multi-Agent-Based Simulation XXI

21st International Workshop, MABS 2020
Auckland, New Zealand, May 10, 2020
Revised Selected Papers

 Springer

Editors
Samarth Swarup (iD)
University of Virginia
Charlottesville, VA, USA

Bastin Tony Roy Savarimuthu (iD)
Department of Information Science
University of Otago
Dunedin, New Zealand

ISSN 0302-9743 ISSN 1611-3349 (electronic)
Lecture Notes in Artificial Intelligence
ISBN 978-3-030-66887-7 ISBN 978-3-030-66888-4 (eBook)
https://doi.org/10.1007/978-3-030-66888-4

LNCS Sublibrary: SL7 – Artificial Intelligence

This Springer imprint is published by the registered company Springer Nature Switzerland AG
The registered company address is: Gewerbestrasse 11, 6330 Cham, Switzerland

Preface

The Multi-Agent-Based Simulation (MABS) Workshop series, which began in 1998, aims to bring together researchers interested in MAS engineering with researchers focused on finding efficient solutions to model complex social systems, in such areas as economics, management, organizational and social sciences in general. Its scientific focus lies at the confluence of social sciences, and multi-agent systems, with a strong application/empirical vein, and its emphasis is on (i) exploratory agent-based simulation as a principled way of undertaking scientific research in the social sciences, and (ii) using social theories as an inspiration for new frameworks and developments in multi-agent systems.

The 21st edition of the workshop, collocated with the 19th International Conference on Autonomous Agents and Multi-Agent Systems (AAMAS), was held virtually (through Zoom) due to the COVID-19 lockdown, on 10th May, 2020. A total of 12 papers were submitted to the workshop and nine were accepted after peer review. These papers were reviewed by two or more PC members using a single-blind review method. This workshop also featured invited talks on the topic of *the role of multi-agent-based simulation in addressing global problems* from Professor Frank Dignum, Dr Maite Lopez-Sanchez, Dr Cristian Jimenez, Dr Mario Paolucci, Dr Jason Thompson, Ms. Fatema T. Johora and Ms. Kaidi Wang. Also, a general discussion centered around the same topic was held. About 25 participants attended the workshop.

This volume represents 8 revised papers (out of 9 accepted for the workshop), which were extended and revised based on the peer reviews received from the workshop. The revisions made to the papers were reviewed by one of the workshop chairs, and this formed the second round of peer review. We are confident this process has resulted in high-quality papers.

The workshop could not have taken place without the contribution of many people. We are very grateful to our invited speakers as well as to all the MABS 2020 participants who took part in the discussions. We are also very grateful to all the members of the Program Committee for their hard work. Thanks also go to Jaime Sichman and Mehdi Dastani (AAMAS 2020 workshop chairs), and to Amal El Fallah Seghrouchni and Gita Sukthankar (AAMAS 2020 general co-chairs). We also thank EasyChair for the use of their conference management system.

November 2020

Samarth Swarup
Bastin Tony Roy Savarimuthu

Organization

Chairs

Samarth Swarup	University of Virginia, USA
Bastin Tony Roy Savarimuthu	University of Otago, New Zealand

Steering Committee

Frédéric Amblard	Toulouse 1 Capitole University, France
Luis Antunes	University of Lisbon, Portugal
Paul Davidsson	Malmö University, Sweden
Nigel Gilbert	University of Surrey, UK
Tim Gulden	George Mason University, USA
Emma Norling	Manchester Metropolitan University, UK
Mario Paolucci	National Research Council, Italy
Jaime Simão Sichman	University of São Paulo, Brazil
Takao Terano	Tokyo Institute of Technology, Japan

Program Committee

Diana Francisca Adamatti	Universidade Federal do Rio Grande, Brazil
Frédéric Amblard	University Toulouse 1 Capitole, France
Luis Antunes	University of Lisbon, Portugal
João Balsa da Silva	University of Lisbon, Portugal
Federico Bianchi	University of Milan, Italy
Sung-Bae Cho	Yonsei University, South Korea
Paul Davidsson	Malmö University, Sweden
Frank Dignum	Umeå University, Sweden
Graçaliz Dimuro	Universidade Federal do Rio Grande, Brazil
Francisco Grimaldo	University of Valencia, Spain
László Gulyás	Eötvös Loránd University, Hungary
Rainer Hegselmann	University of Bayreuth, Germany
Ruth Meyer	Manchester Metropolitan University, UK
Jean-Pierre Müller	CIRAD, France
Luis Gustavo Nardin	National College of Ireland, Ireland
Paulo Novais	University of Minho, Portugal
Mario Paolucci	Institute of Cognitive Sciences & Technologies, Italy
William Rand	North Carolina State University, USA
Juliette Rouchier	CNRS-LAMSADE, France
Klaus G. Troitzsch	University of Koblenz-Landau, Germany
Natalie van der Wal	Delft University of Technology, The Netherlands

| Harko Verhagen | Stockholm University, Sweden |
| Neil Yorke-Smith | Delft University of Technology, The Netherlands |

Additional Reviewers

Leonardo Emmendorfer
Chathika Gunaratne
Chathura Jayalath

Contents

Adaptivity in Distributed Agent-Based Simulation: A Generic Load-
Balancing Approach 1
   Stig Bosmans, Toon Bogaerts, Wim Casteels, Siegfried Mercelis,
   Joachim Denil, and Peter Hellinckx

Trajectory Modelling in Shared Spaces: Expert-Based vs. Deep
Learning Approach? 13
   Hao Cheng, Fatema T. Johora, Monika Sester, and Jörg P. Müller

Towards Agent-Based Traffic Simulation Using Live Data from Sensors
for Smart Cities 28
   Yan Qian, Johan Barthelemy, and Pascal Perez

Design and Evaluations of Multi-agent Simulation Model for Electric
Power Sharing Among Households 41
   Yasutaka Nishimura, Taichi Shimura, Kiyoshi Izumi,
   and Kiyohito Yoshihara

Active Screening on Recurrent Diseases Contact Networks with
Uncertainty: A Reinforcement Learning Approach. 54
   Han Ching Ou, Kai Wang, Finale Doshi-Velez, and Milind Tambe

Impact of Meta-roles on the Evolution of Organisational Institutions 66
   Amir Hosein Afshar Sedigh, Martin K. Purvis,
   Bastin Tony Roy Savarimuthu, Maryam A. Purvis,
   and Christopher K. Frantz

Optimization of Large-Scale Agent-Based Simulations Through Automated
Abstraction and Simplification 81
   Alexey Tregubov and Jim Blythe

Improved Travel Demand Modeling with Synthetic Populations 94
   Kaidi Wang, Wenwen Zhang, Henning Mortveit, and Samarth Swarup

Author Index 107

Adaptivity in Distributed Agent-Based Simulation: A Generic Load-Balancing Approach

Stig Bosmans[1(✉)], Toon Bogaerts[1], Wim Casteels[1], Siegfried Mercelis[1],
Joachim Denil[2], and Peter Hellinckx[1]

[1] IDLab - Faculty of Applied Engineering, University of Antwerp - Imec,
Sint -Pietersvliet 7, 2000 Antwerp, Belgium
{stig.bosmans,toon.bogaerts,wim.casteels,siegfried.mercelis,
peter.hellinckx}@uantwerpen.be
[2] Flanders Make, University of Antwerp,
Groenenborgerlaan 171, 2020 Antwerp, Belgium
joachim.denil@uantwerpen.be

Abstract. Distributed agent-based simulations often suffer from an imbalance in computational load, leading to a suboptimal use of resources. This happens when part of the computational resoures are waiting idle for another process to finish. Self-adaptive load-balancing algorithms have been developed to use these resources more optimally. These algorithms are typically implemented ad-hoc, making re-usability and maintenance difficult. In this work, we present a generic self-adaptive framework. This methodology is evaluated with the Acsim framework on two simulations: a micro-traffic simulation and a cellular automata simulation. For each of these scenarios a scalable and adaptive load-balancing algorithm is implemented, showing significant improvements in execution time of the simulation.

Keywords: Distributed agent-based simulation · Adaptivity ·
MAPE-K · Dynamic load balancing

1 Introduction

Although Agent-Based Simulation (ABS) is a relatively new simulation paradigm [16], it has been used as an effective tool in a wide range of research domains [1,2,4,20]. The main characteristic in ABS is the concept of an agent, which is a self-contained autonomous entity, with the ability to interact with other agents and with the environment. These interactions can lead to complex emergent behavior [6]. Agent-Based Simulation is, therefore, one of the most powerful and natural tools to simulate emergent phenomena using a bottom-up approach.

ABS has been used to evaluate and analyze behavior of complex large-scale dynamic systems such as traffic systems [1] or complex Internet of Things systems such as smart city environments [4]. However, traditional monolithic ABS simulations quickly run into problems when the scale of the simulation increases.

© Springer Nature Switzerland AG 2021
S. Swarup and B. T. R. Savarimuthu (Eds.): MABS 2020, LNAI 12316, pp. 1–12, 2021.
https://doi.org/10.1007/978-3-030-66888-4_1

This is the case This becomes especially problematic when the application of these simulations is time-critical. Therefore, reducing the computational cost and the run-time of these simulations is vital.

With this motivation, researchers have replaced the classic monolithic set-up by a distributed architecture. This can be achieved by partitioning the simulation into separate logical processes. This allows the simulation to be divided among multiple processors and servers, thus allowing to simulate larger systems and reducing the simulation run-time. This however also increases the complexity and may add inefficiencies such as the need for synchronization and slow remote communication between simulation partitions. Furthermore, the inherently dynamic aspect of agent-based simulation makes static partitioning inefficient because the computational load of each process changes during the simulation. This can lead to a significant waste of resources, for example, the simulation can start perfectly balanced, but over time the distribution of these agents can become highly imbalanced. Such distribution imbalance is often due to agents that change their locations, increase communications or change their internal load. A direct consequence of such imbalances is a significant increase in run-time and under-utilization of computational resources. As stated by Long et al. it is likely that such load imbalances occur in distributed agent-based simulations [15].

In this paper, we propose to organize the distribution adaptively by dynamically reacting to imbalances in computational load, synchronization load, and communication load. Most state-of-the-art load-balancing mechanisms are implemented in an ad-hoc manner, making them hard to reuse and maintain. The contribution of this paper is a generic framework to implement self-adaptivity in distributed agent-based simulators. We evaluate this method using two different implementations: a large-scale micro-traffic simulation with a graph-based environment and a cellular automata simulation with the Sugarscape model.

The second section of this paper discusses the concept of adaptivity and related work. Section three presents the architecture of the distributed agent-based simulation framework Acsim, that will be used to evaluate the experiments. Section four presents the main principles of a MAPE-K loop and its implementation in Acsim. Section five presents the specific examples and the conclusions are drawn in Sect. 6.

2   Adaptivity in Agent-Based Simulation

Adaptivity in agent-based simulations can be related to the notion of activity which was introduced by Muzy et al. as a measure of the number of events occurring during a discrete event simulation [18]. As stated by Y. Van Tendeloo et al. activity can be interpreted depending on the particular resource one wishes to focus on (time, memory, energy,..) [23]. Therefore both the communicational load and the computational load can be seen as types of 'activity'. For example, from a communicational load perspective, an agent has high activity if it generates many messages in a fixed time window. From the computational load perspective, an agent has high activity if its step duration takes a long time to process.

Given this definition of activity, we can go ahead and define adaptivity as the property of a distributed simulation framework to dynamically react to imbalances of activity with the aim to restore the balance and improve overall simulation run-time.

Adaptivity is typically implemented as a load balancing optimization problem based on global information [5,24]. The activity is defined as a function of computational load, synchronization load and communication load. The disadvantage of these approaches is that they require global information to be stored or synchronized centrally and that the optimization algorithm is computationally intensive and thus less scalable. It is also possible to use heuristics that only require local information, making these solutions computationally much more efficient, but the obtained optimum might be local. For example, D'Angelo et al. present in their work a range of heuristics that trigger agent migrations based on local and remote communication patterns [8] and Q. Long et al. present a distributed load balancing algorithm based on partial local information [15].

But adaptivity is not constrained to solving load balancing problems only. In [10] and [3] the authors show that adaptivity can be used to dynamically switch abstraction levels of a single agent or a collection of agents. Switching to a higher abstraction level leads to a reduction in the computational load at the cost of losing accuracy.

Most of the related work rely on ad-hoc implementations of adaptivity. An exception is the work of Franceschini et al. who are using a MAPE-K control loop to implement an automatic simulation abstraction solution [10]. In the following sections, we expand on this work and present the integration of a MAPE-K control loop in the Acsim distributed simulation framework. Furthermore, we show that MAPE-K can also be used effectively for adaptive load-balancing.

3   Distributed Simulation Architecture: Acsim

Acsim is a distributed Python-based agent-based framework, developed by the authors, inspired by Mesa [17]. It has been developed as a prototyping simulation framework. The goal of the framework is not to be a production-ready simulation framework but to allow for the validation of state-of-the-art techniques regarding simulation scalability. We hope that these techniques will eventually inspire production-ready distributed agent-based simulation frameworks.

One of the main motivations for the development of Acsim is the observation that there is an increasing need for large scale simulators in the context of Internet of Things (IoT) and Smart Traffic applications. Due to the increase of connectivity of smart devices and the availability of real-time data, simulation platforms provide the opportunity to simulate entire cities. Simulation technology enables the creation of a virtual testbed of large-scale IoT applications and allows for real-time simulation-based optimization. An application of this technology is, for example, a real-time city-wide and simulation-based traffic light optimization platform. But state-of-the-art simulators are limited in their scalability capabilities to support such technology. This is the challenge that Acsim tackles. Although Acsim focuses on large scale IoT and traffic simulation, it can also support other agent-based simulations.

Acsim relies on a conservative time-stepped synchronization mechanism. Where time is collectively progressed after the completion of each individual agent step. The architecture of the simulator is displayed in Fig. 1. Acsim consists of three main building blocks: 1) Agent: represents an entity at its highest granularity, an agent contains a state, can adapt its state at each time-step and has the possibility to interact with other agents using message-passing and interact with the environment. 2) Model: a model serves as a container for a specific type of agent and is responsible for the initialization of all agents of this type. For example, a class of car agents will be part of a car model. This car model will initialize all cars, generate routes and collects car-related logging information. 3) Logical Processes: Acsim consists of multiple sub-simulator or LP's. Each LP manages a part of the environment and a collection of agents that are located in this partial environment. It runs a dedicated process and is responsible for low-level simulation tasks such as handling agent migrations, managing message-passing between local and remote agents, collecting logs and initiating agent steps. An agent step is a discrete step forward in time. Only as part of a step can an agent adapt its state or communicate with other agents and the environment. The global synchronization is managed by the master coordinator. The coordinator orders all LP's to execute the next step. Furthermore, the coordinator collects and stores logs generated by the LP's. Finally, Acsim has extensive monitoring capabilities, enabling an in-depth analysis of local and global simulator performance.

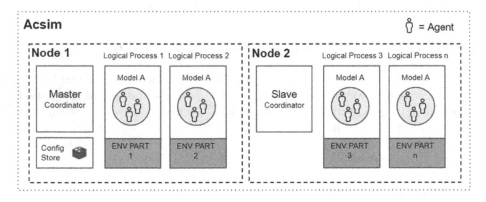

Fig. 1. Acsim - Distributed simulator architecture. Acsim contains a cluster of nodes and a node represents a physical device with one or more CPU cores, connected to other nodes via the network.

4   MAPE-K as a Generic Framework for Adaptivity

Due to the ever-increasing complexity of computing infrastructure, a shift to self-managing systems is observed in the field of software development. In 2005, IBM introduced MAPE-K loops to deal with this complexity [11]. Measure Analyze Plan Execute - Knowledge (MAPE-K) loops are closed feedback loops which can handle the complexities of self-adaptivity. More recently, [12] described templates on how to utilize MAPE-K control loops to different distributed applications. The implementation of most adaptive optimization strategies in a simulation is ad-hoc and cannot be reused efficiently. We propose the application of a MAPE-K control loop as a generic solution that will allow existing adaptivity strategies to be efficiently implemented and maintained.

As mentioned above, the Acsim framework is step-based which results in the simulation being as fast as the slowest simulator in the distribution. There is no guarantee that this local optimization leads to a global optimum. The overhead of calculating the global optimum, at a master node, increases with the scale of the simulation. Because of the varying load-distribution over time, the global optimum shifts and a new optimization iteration is needed. Our approach focuses on a distributed solution to partitioning/merging environments. Our approach is generic, each simulator can easily implement its specific logic as part of the MAPE-K framework implemented in Acsim. Execution of the MAPE-K loop is handled by the Acsim framework. We put extra emphasis during development that the MAPE-K framework is implemented in a modular way, as part of the simulation coordination engine. Its architecture can therefore be transferred to most agent-based simulators and be integrated without significant changes. This is because the MAPE-K framework breaks the barrier between simulation application and simulation engine. We can refer to this as leaky abstraction. This design choice has been made in order for the framework to be implemented in other simulation engines without breaking existing simulation applications. The trade-off however is that a simulation application developer needs to be aware of low-level aspects of the simulation engine when developing a MAPE-K implementation for its application. Next, we will go in-depth on the structure of the MAPE-K framework integrated into Acsim:

1. **Monitor**: During this phase, logs are retrieved from each subpart of the Acsim framework regarding the model, simulator and environment. When a MAPE-K iteration starts these logs are stored to the shared knowledge. This knowledge base is located at the master node. To enhance the scalability, only low compute algorithms are used at the master level.
2. **Analyze**: This has access to the shared knowledge base to identify bottlenecks and flag optimization opportunities. These identifications do not provide a solution but an indication of the performance of a certain entity in the framework.
3. **Plan**: This step collects all flags and generates an optimization plan without execution. There could be multiple optimization plans in a single MAPE-K loop.

4. **Execute**: This phase of the loop runs distributed after receiving an optimization request from the planning phase. This phase has the highest computation
   requirement in the loop. The optimization algorithms used can vary from each
   application. When a local optimization is complete, a synchronization message is sent to all relevant entities involved in the optimization.
5. **Knowledge**: This part is shared between the first three steps of the loop.
   The execute step does not need the knowledge base as it only executes the
   plans created during the previous step. During each iteration, the knowledge
   can be expanded to store relevant information for future MAPE-K loops.

Each simulation will have access to the simulation logs, these are stored in
the knowledge class. The MAPE-K framework implemented in Acsim allows
easy implementation of the phases and allow for reuseable, maintaineable and
application-specific adaptivity behavior. The loop can be executed both locally
and centrally. Also a hierarchy of multiple loops, affecting each other is supported
by the framework.

5   Motivating Examples

In the previous sections we introduced the concept of adaptivity and how we can
implement it generically in the Acsim framework using the MAPE-K framework.
In this section we validate this approach on two different agent-based simulations.
In both scenarios we implement a novel activity load balancing heuristics. As
stated in Sect. 4, we differentiate compared to classical adaptive load balancing
algorithms by making sure the heuristics are not performed centrally but at the
level of a LP to ensure scalability. In the experiments our aim is to improve
the global step duration GSD of the entire simulation. We can express it as
follows: $GSD = max_i(LSD^i)$, where LSD^i is the local step duration of LP i.
In other words, the global step duration is always equal to the worst LP step
duration. The reason for this is that Acsim relies on a conservative time-stepped
synchronization algorithm, as discussed in Sect. 3. In the examples below the
goal is to improve the activity balance with each MAPE-K iteration. To gain
insight in how LP's are performing, we distinguish the different contributions to
the step duration (as discussed in detail in [8]): the Model Computation Cost
(MCC), the Remote Communication Cost (RCC), the Local Communication
Cost (LCC) and the Model Synchronisation Cost (MSC). The weight of each
contribution is application-specific. When an imbalance occurs, for each variable
a different optimization strategy could be used. When optimizing on a local level,
each LP calculates their cost balance using only local information.

5.1   Adaptive Local Optimization of Compute Cost - A Micro-traffic
Example

In this example we perform a micro-traffic simulation of a 20 km by 20 km urban
area where cars are making random trips. Each car is an agent, managing its state

and adapting its acceleration based on speed regulation and the acceleration of leading cars. The implemented models are based on the Intelligent Driver Model [22], which is a state-of-the-art car following model and the lane-changing model MOBIL (Minimizing Overall Braking Induced By Lane Changing) [14]. This implementation leads to both realistic local behavior and realistic emerging behavior. All cars comply to standard traffic regulations and priority rules.

The environment is represented by a directed graph datastructure. Edges are roads (with single or more lanes) and nodes are junctions. A car agent can interact with the environment by requesting where nearby cars are located. Car agents can also interact with each-other to request acceleration and related information or with traffic light agents to request the state of a traffic light.

During initialization the environment is partitioned based on the number of available cores. The partitioning algorithm is a multilevel recursive algorithm for multi-constraint graph partitioning as presented [13]. It attempts to balance node cost of the graph partitions and minimizes edge cut. A single LP will manage a single environment partition and the agents located in this partition. When agents leave the environment partition they will migrate to a simulator that manages one of the neighboring partitions. At the edges of a partition, car agents require state information of agents that are located in the neighbouring partition. Therefore, we include a synchronization mechanism. This mechanism broadcasts the state of an agent, located at a border area, to neighboring partitions after each state update. In this scenario the cost of a step depends on two activity parameters: Model Computation Cost, MCC and Model Synchronization Cost MSC. In the remainder of this section we elaborate on how we can dynamically load balance these activity parameters using local information only in order to reduce the global step duration.

Optimization Algorithm: A significant amount of research has been done in the context of distributed micro-traffic simulation. The load balancing problem is one of the most discussed problems within this context. As stated in [19] it is necessary for all simulation processes to consume similar amount of computing power in order to run at the same speed and the communication among the processes should be minimal. Ramamohanar et al. [21] introduce a spatial workload balancing approach where they partition the environment in grids. As pointed out by the authors, this approach is static, and unable to react to changes in computational load introduced by agent migrations. Cordasco et al. presented a distributed extension to the Agent-Based Simulation framework MASON [7]. In their work to put extra emphasis to the partitioning and load balancing problem. But also their implementation is not generic nor dynamic. Instead, other work, such as Xu et al.'s work that presents an adaptive graph partitioning approach [24]. They essentially execute the graph partitioning algorithm multiple times, on the entire traffic network, when imbalances are detected. The problem with this approach is that the algorithm runs on the entire network, making a distributed approach difficult.

To solve this problem, we propose a heuristic-based approach, powered by the MAPE-K framework presented in the previous section, that is able to run in a distributed way. The global idea of the algorithm is that we keep track of activity using an activity graph. For example, assuming car agent computational load is homogeneous, we keep track of the number of cars located on the incoming edges of a node. When imbalances are detected between neighboring environment partitions we allow an overloaded partition to migrate a collection of its border nodes and edges to a neighboring, less occupied partition. This is visualized in Fig. 2. The amount of nodes and edges that gets migrated depends on the amount of activity that needs to be transferred in order to reestablish the activity balance.

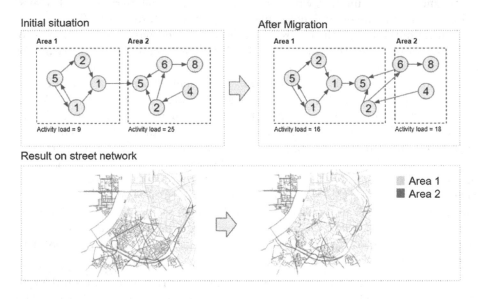

Fig. 2. Heuristic: Load balancing using local activity graphs

Experiment: The implementation of the computational load balance algorithm in the MAPE-K framework is explained below:

1. **Monitor**: We keep track of the global step duration (GSD) and the local step durations of the simulators (LSD^i).
2. **Analyze**: The average LSD is calculated. When one of the LSD exceeds the average by 20% or more, the algorithm evaluates if part of the computational activity can be offloaded to the neighbors (this is achieved by migrating nodes, edges and agents). If this is the case a 'migration flag' is set.
3. **Plan**: When a migration flag is found, a plan of execution will be created. This plan orders the overloaded area to migrate a given amount of activity to one of its neighboring areas that has been selected in the Analyze step.
4. **Execute**: The overloaded area will calculate which nodes it can offload. Consequently, both the originating area and the destination area will update their graph datastructure accordingly.

We ran an experiment to test this implementation. In the experiment we randomly generate trips in a city center. We introduced an initial imbalance of 1/10. This could be a realistic scenario when people are leaving a residential area to an industrial area in the morning. We expect the algorithm to restore this imbalance over time. Thirty runs of this experiment were executed, the average and standard error are displayed in Fig. 3. In both graphs we compare a non-adaptive approach with an adaptive approach. The MAPE-K optimization is performed at time-step 250. Note that this time-step has been chosen based on the application related observations and requirements. As this is mostly a domain-specific decision, the time-step interval can be easily adapted by the simulation developer. We observe a significant reduction of step duration when the optimization occurs.

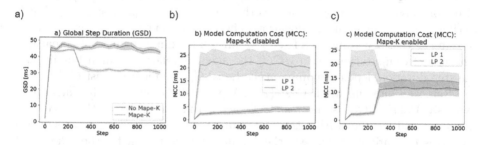

Fig. 3. Results - with and without MAPE-K adaptive optimization, micro-traffic simulation

Balancing Synchronization Cost: As explained in the introduction, the step duration not only depends on Model Computation Cost (MCC). It also depends on Model Synchronization Cost (MSC). The impact largely depends on the scenario. When there is a large amount of traffic at the border areas of environment partitions, the MSC will be significant and cannot be ignored. Therefore, further optimization will be required. We propose a technique that can be explored in future work. The general idea is that we can measure the synchronization cost based on the amount of agents located in a border area. When an imbalance in synchronization cost is observed between areas, we can simulate the synchronization cost after incremental expansion of the graph. This is similar to incremental expansion demonstrated in Fig. 2. When the synchronization cost of the incremental expansion is lower than the initial cost, we can perform a migration of nodes and edges.

In conclusion, the proposed synchronization heuristic combined with the computational cost balancing heuristic we expect it to lead to a further reduction in step duration. The proposed heuristics will improve upon sub-optimal scenarios where imbalances are observed in neighboring areas, in a scalable and computationally efficient manner. But, it is limited to finding local optimal solutions, not a global optimal solution.

5.2   Adaptive Local Optimization of Communication Cost - A Cellular Automata Example

In this example we use the agent-based simulation Sugarscape [9] with a cellular automata environment. This example was chosen as it is a well-known agent-based simulation and because the type of the environment Sugarscape uses is used by many other agent-based simulators. This shows that ideas presented here are transferable to similar agent-based simulations. These simulations typically lead to emergent behaviour and can be used in, for example, biology [2]. In Sugarscape, sugar is grown in each cell of the environment at a certain rate and the goal of the agents is to survive by collecting enough sugar. If an agent cannot satisfy his metabolism, he is replaced by a randomly initiated agent at a random vacant position. The agents are characterised by a metabolic rate and range of sight. At each step they search for sugar by looking in the four perpendicular directions and move one step towards the cell with the highest sugar level, collecting the sugar at their new location. The environment regrows sugar at each step in the cells according to a fixed rate until a maximal sugar level is reached. The model computation cost (MCC) the agent is relatively small but instead the step duration depends mainly on the Local Communicaton Cost (LCC) and the Remote Communication Cost (RCC) (with RCC being significantly more expensive). The RCC is the result of agents that are close to the edge of a simulator and searches within the next simulator for sugar. This consists of two messages that are send between the simulators: one to ask for the amount of sugar on the cells of interest and one with the corresponding answer. Our optimization algorithm keeps track of a communication based activity graph, where imbalances in LCC and RCC between simulators are monitored and dynamically improved by migrating parts of the environment. The MAPE-K cycle is implemented as follows:

1. **Monitor**: The local and remote (both contributions due to received and send messages) compute time for each cell is logged.
2. **Analyze**: Bottleneck simulators are identified by comparing their Local Step Duration (LSD) to the Global Step Duration (GSD).
3. **Plan**: A plan is created to partition certain sections of the simulator's environment to restore imbalances that might have manifested over time. Each section is evaluated using its logged LCC and RCC. During partitioning, the algorithm can decide to migrate a section which will switch LCC to RCC (and possibly vice versa), and as a consequence reduce overall cost.
4. **Execute**: Each simulator executes his part of the established plan and possibly migrates parts of its environment to another simulation process.

To evaluate the performance of the adaptive approach, we ran 30 random initiated Sugarscape simulations and compared them to 30 non-adaptive simulations. Both simulations are initiated with four LP's managing each a quarter of the environment. The simulation stops after 800 steps, the MAPE-k framework is executed every 50th step. The results are illustrated in Fig. 4. Image a represent the initiated environment divided over the four LP's. Figure Image b shows the same environment where the borders are optimized based on the current activity. Finally, c illustrates the average step duration and the standard error. From

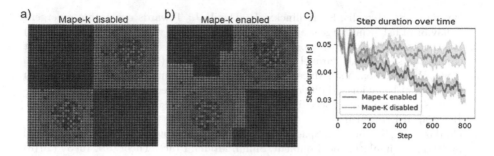

Fig. 4. Results - with and without MAPE-K adaptive optimization, Sugarscape.

these results we can see that once the random activity of the agents is replaced with emerging behaviour, the adaptive approach improves performance.

6   Conclusion

In this work we presented a MAPE-K loop as a generic and effective framework to implement a self-adaptive distribution for agent-based simulations. We evaluated this framework by implementing two examples: a distributed traffic simulation and a sugarscape simulation. We showed that MAPE-K can be used effictively in multiple simulations to implement adaptivity. Furthermore, the results of the proposed adaptive load-balancing heuristics show a significant reduction in computational cost while being executed decentralized. In future work we will further optimize the presented heuristics and perform an empirical comparison with MAPE-K implementations of state-of-the-art load-balancing techniques. Furthermore, we want to explore the benefits of a hybrid decentralized and centralized adaptive load balancing approach in micro traffic simulation. In this hybrid scenario we envision two MAPE-K loops: 1) a decentralized heuristic, as proposed in this paper, and 2) a centralized load balancing algorithm that is able to find global optimum, as proposed in the related work of Sect. 5.1. We also want to validate the generality of the approach by implementing the MAPE-K approach in other distributed simulation frameworks.

References

1. Balmer, M., Cetin, N., Nagel, K., Raney, B.: Towards truly agent-based traffic and mobility simulations. In: Proceedings of the Third International Joint Conference on Autonomous Agents and Multiagent Systems, AAMAS 2004, pp. 60–67. IEEE (2004)
2. Baradaran, S., Maleknasr, N., Setayeshi, S., Akbari, M.E.: Prediction of lung cells oncogenic transformation for induced radon progeny alpha particles using sugarscape cellular automata. Iran. J. Cancer Prevent. **7**(1), 40 (2014)
3. Bosmans, S., Mercelis, S., Hellinckx, P., Denil, J.: Reducing computational cost of large-scale simulations using opportunistic model approximation. In: 2019 Spring Simulation Conference (SpringSim), pp. 1–12 (2019)

4. Bosmans, S., Mercelis, S., Hellinckx, P., Denil, J.: Towards evaluating emergent behavior of IoT using large scale simulation techniques (wip). In: Springsim (2018)
5. Boukerche, A.: An adaptive partitioning algorithm for distributed discrete event simulation systems. J. Parallel Distrib. Comput. **62**(9) (2002)
6. Chan, W.K.V., Son, Y.J., Macal, C.M.: Agent-based simulation tutorial-simulation of emergent behavior and differences between agent-based simulation and discrete-event simulation. In: Proceedings of the 2010 winter simulation conference, pp. 135–150. IEEE (2010)
7. Cordasco, G., Scarano, V., Spagnuolo, C.: Distributed mason: a scalable distributed multi-agent simulation environment. Simul. Model. Pract. Theor. **89**, 15–34 (2018)
8. D'Angelo, G.: The simulation model partitioning problem: an adaptive solution based on self-clustering. Simul. Model. Pract. Theor. **70**, 1–20 (2017)
9. Epstein, J.M., Axtell, R.: Growing Artificial Societies: Social Science from the Bottom up. Brookings Institution Press, Washington, D.C (1996)
10. Franceschini, R., Challenger, M., Cicchetti, A., Denil, J., Vangheluwe, H.: Challenges for automation in adaptive abstraction. In: 2019 ACM/IEEE 22nd International Conference on MDE Languages and Systems Companion (MODELS-C). IEEE (2019)
11. IBM: An architectural blueprint for autonomic computing (2006)
12. Iglesia, D.G.D.L., Weyns, D.: Mape-k formal templates to rigorously design behaviors for self-adaptive systems. ACM TAAS **10**(3), 1–31 (2015)
13. Karypis, G., Kumar, V.: Multilevel algorithms for multi-constraint graph partitioning. In: SC 1998: Proceedings of the 1998 ACM/IEEE Conference on Supercomputing, pp. 28–28. IEEE (1998)
14. Kesting, A., Treiber, M., Helbing, D.: General lane-changing model mobile for car-following models. Trans. Res. Rec. **1999**(1), 86–94 (2007)
15. Long, Q., Lin, J., Sun, Z.: Agent scheduling model for adaptive dynamic load balancing in agent-based distributed simulations. Simul. Model. Pract. Theor. **19**(4), 1021–1034 (2011)
16. Macal, C.M., North, M.J.: Tutorial on agent-based modeling and simulation. In: Proceedings of the Winter Simulation Conference 2005, pp. 14-pp. IEEE (2005)
17. Masad, D., Kazil, J.: Mesa: an agent-based modeling framework. In: 14th PYTHON in Science Conference, pp. 53–60 (2015)
18. Muzy, A., Touraille, L., Vangheluwe, H., Michel, O., Traoré, M.K., Hill, D.R.: Activity regions for the specification of discrete event systems. In: Proceedings of the 2010 Spring Simulation Multiconference, pp. 1–7 (2010)
19. Potuzak, T.: Distributed traffic simulation and the reduction of inter-process communication using traffic flow characteristics transfer. In: Tenth International Conference on Computer Modeling and Simulation, pp. 525–530. IEEE (2008)
20. Raberto, M., Cincotti, S., Focardi, S.M., Marchesi, M.: Agent-based simulation of a financial market. Stat. Mech. Appl. **299**, 1–2 (2001)
21. Ramamohanarao, K., et. al.: Smarts: scalable microscopic adaptive road traffic simulator. ACM TIST, **8**(2), 1–22 (2016)
22. Treiber, M., Kesting, A.: Traffic Flow Dynamics. Data, Models and Simulation. Springer-Verlag, Berlin Heidelberg (2013)
23. Van Tendeloo, Y., Vangheluwe, H.: Activity in pythonpdevs. In: ITM Web of Conferences.-Place of publication unknown, vol. 3, p. 01002 (2014)
24. Xu, Y., Cai, W., Aydt, H., Lees, M.: Efficient graph-based dynamic load-balancing for parallel large-scale agent-based traffic sim. In: WinterSim. IEEE (2014)

Trajectory Modelling in Shared Spaces: Expert-Based vs. Deep Learning Approach?

Hao Cheng[1]([✉]), Fatema T. Johora[2], Monika Sester[1], and Jörg P. Müller[2]

[1] Institute of Cartography and Geoinformatics, Leibniz University Hannover,
Appel-Str. 9a, 30167 Hanover, Germany
{Hao.Cheng,Monika.Sester}@ikg.uni-hannover.de
[2] Department of Informatics, Clausthal University of Technology,
Julius-Albert-Str. 4, 38678 Clausthal-Zellerfeld, Germany
{fatema.tuj.johora,joerg.mueller}@tu-clausthal.de

Abstract. Realistically modelling behaviour and interaction of hetero-geneous road users (pedestrians and vehicles) in mixed-traffic zones (a.k.a. shared spaces) is challenging. The dynamic nature of the environment, heterogeneity of transport modes, and the absence of classical traffic rules make realistic microscopic traffic simulation hard problems. Existing multi-agent-based simulations of shared spaces largely use an expert-based approach, combining a symbolic (e.g. rule-based) modelling and reasoning paradigm (e.g. using BDI representations of beliefs and plans) with the hand-crafted encoding of the actual decision logic. More recently, deep learning (DL) models are largely used to derive and predict trajectories based on e.g. video data. In-depth studies comparing these two kinds of approaches are missing. In this work, we propose an expert-based model called *GSFM* that combines Social Force Model and Game theory and a DL model called *LSTM-DBSCAN* that manipulates Long Short-Term Memories and density-based clustering for multi-agent trajectory prediction. We create a common framework to run these two models in parallel to guarantee a fair comparison. Real-world mixed traffic data from shared spaces of different layout are used to calibrate/train and evaluate the models. The empirical results imply that both models can generate realistic predictions, but they differ in the way of handling collisions and mimicking heterogeneous behaviour. Via a thorough study, we draw the conclusion of their respective strengths and weaknesses.

Keywords: Mixed-traffic interaction · Deep learning · Game theory

Supported by the German Research Foundation (DFG) through the Research Training Group SocialCars (GRK 1931). The authors thank the participants of the DFG research project MODIS (DFG project #248905318) for providing data sets.
F.T. Johora and H. Cheng—Contribute equally to this work.

S. Swarup and B. T. R. Savarimuthu (Eds.): MABS 2020, LNAI 12316, pp. 13–27, 2021.
https://doi.org/10.1007/978-3-030-66888-4_2

1   Introduction

In comparison to conventional traffic design where road resources are allocated to road users (agents) by time or space segregation, *shared space* largely removes road signs, signals, and markings, forcing direct interaction between mixed traffic participants (e.g. cars, bikes, pedestrians), guided by informal social protocols and negotiation. This concept was first introduced by Monderman in the 1970s [9]. Shared spaces nowadays can be found in urban areas of many European cities; examples are the Laweiplein intersection in the Dutch town Drachten, Skvallertorget in Norrköping, and Kensington High Street in London [14].

The absence of explicit traffic rules and thereby caused vagueness make it critical to investigate safety issues, especially regarding vulnerable road users (i.e. pedestrians) and traffic efficiency of shared spaces [14]. The foreseeable advent of autonomous driving also raises the need for automated safety systems based on the intent recognition of other road users [11]. However, understanding how road users behave and predicting their actions is far from trivial as these actions are a result of complex decision-making processes from heterogeneous road users.

There is a considerable body of research on microscopic models aimed at tackling these challenges. In particular, we can distinguish two classes of methodologies: the so-called *expert-based* approaches [4,15,19,25,28,31,34] and *data-driven* approaches [2,7,8,13,17,23,29]. Expert-based approaches involve human designers to craft explicit decision rules and corresponding reasoning mechanism to tackle the modelling problem. For example, in the Social Force Model (SFM) [15], the rules of physical dynamics are used to mimic pedestrian movement behaviour in crowded space. Game theory has been used in interaction modelling e.g., users negotiating the right-of-way [5,19,31]. However, the requirement of human intervention makes it difficult to scale these models for large or new problems. On the other hand, *data-driven modelling approaches* can be trained by processing the data extracted from real-world situations and deriving a complex neural network structure with associated parameters or weights optimised via training [22]. Examples are e.g. Social-LSTM [2] and Social-GAN [13]. These models are often black boxes, making them hard to understand and explain for humans; The human modeller's intention to guide the models to capture specific desired patterns is difficult to support [16]. Up to now, there is no easy way to interpret the latent features used by a DL model, especially when the structure is of very high dimensionality. Thus, a lack of reliable control of the model may lead to faulty or counter-intuitive behaviour. Besides, computational cost can be a bottleneck for DL-based models [30].

However, it is not easy to fairly compare the expert-based and DL approaches in modelling and predicting mixed traffic trajectories. Firstly, it is difficult to create a common framework that both models can share for a fair comparison. Moreover, they may have different criteria in terms of performance. As an example, expert approaches focus on generating realistic trajectories for agents in simulation, while data-driven approaches focus on predicting trajectories as close as possible to the real trajectories, the so-called ground truth. Hence, the input and output of these approaches are often different.

To our knowledge, there are no studies that compare expert-based and DL approaches for microscopically modelling complex socio-technical systems, namely, shared spaces. Our contributions are summarised below:

- We pursue two models: an expert-based (GSFM, combining a game-theoretic and physics-based model) and a DL model (LSTM-DBSCAN, Long Short-Term Memories with Density-Based Spatial Clustering of Applications with Noise [10]).
- We create a common framework for a fair comparison. These two models take the same data as input and generate predictions in the same format.
- The accuracy (in terms of realistic behaviour) of these two models is tested on real-world shared-space scenarios using the same evaluation metrics. Their strengths and weaknesses are experimentally compared and analysed.

2 Methodology

2.1 Problem Formulation

The prediction task is to generate realistic and collision-free future trajectories of the vehicle and pedestrian agents in shared spaces. As preparation for empirical data, all the trajectories with discrete time steps of $0.5\,\mathrm{s}$ e.g. $(x_i^t, y_i^t) \in \mathbb{R}^2$ on a 2D plane are received from video sequences recorded by static cameras, where x and y are pixel coordinates for the given video, which can be easily converted to meters using the given scale, i stands for agent ID and t for time step. The time steps in observation are $\{1, \cdots, k\}$ and the time steps in prediction are $\{k+1, \cdots, m\}$. Accordingly, the visible trajectories for N agents are denoted as $\mathbf{X} = X_1, X_2, ..., X_n$, where $X_i = \sum_{t=1}^{k}(x_i^t, y_i^t)$ and $i \in N$. The prediction of the future trajectories are $\hat{\mathbf{Y}} = \hat{Y_1}, \hat{Y_2}, ..., \hat{Y_n}$, respectively. The task is to predict each agent's location at prediction time steps based on the locations at observation time steps for both DL and expert-based models. Thus, the objective is to minimise $L(\mathbf{Y}, \hat{\mathbf{Y}})$, where $\hat{\mathbf{Y}} = f(\mathbf{X})$ and $\mathbf{Y}$ is the ground truth, $f(.)$ stands for the prediction models, and $L(.,.)$ the loss function.

2.2 Game-Theoretic Social Force Model

We pursue an expert-based approach, called Game-Theoretic Social Force Model (GSFM) [19]. In GSFM, the movement of each agent is modelled in three modules: *trajectory planning, force-based modelling*, and *game-theoretic decision-making*. Each module has different roles to perform. GSFM is built on a BDI (**B**elief, **D**esire, **I**ntention) platform, LightJason [3], to design and explain the control flow among the modules. The BDI controller acts as the brain of the agent to perceive the environment and activate one of these modules based on the situation. Each module triggers the controller on the completion of their respective task(s). Figure 1 visualises the overall structure of the GSFM model. The trajectory planning module computes free-flow trajectories for each agent by considering static obstacles like boundaries, or trees in the shared space. The force-based modelling and game-theoretic decision modules are responsible for modelling interactions among agents. In GSFM, these interactions are classified into two categories based on the observation of the video data and on the classification of road users' behaviour given by Helbing et al. [15]: simple interaction (percept → act) and complex interaction (percept → choose an action among many alternatives → act).

The force-based module handles simple interactions. It uses the classical SFM to capture the driving force of each agent (i) towards their destination $(\boldsymbol{D}_i^o)$, the repulsive force from static obstacle $(\boldsymbol{I}_{iW})$ and from other pedestrian $(\boldsymbol{I}_{ij})$, to the target agent, and extends SFM to capture car following interaction $(\boldsymbol{I}_{\text{following}})$ and pedestrian-to-vehicle reactive interaction $(\boldsymbol{I}_{\text{stopping}})$.

$$\boldsymbol{D}_i^o = \frac{\boldsymbol{v}^*_i(t) - \boldsymbol{v}_i(t)}{\tau}, \tag{1}$$

$$\boldsymbol{I}_{ij} = V_{ij}^o \exp\left[\frac{-\boldsymbol{d}_{ij}(t)}{\sigma}\right] \hat{n}_{ij} F_{ij}, \tag{2}$$

$$\boldsymbol{I}_{iW} = U_{iW}^o \exp\left[\frac{-\boldsymbol{d}_{iW}(t)}{R}\right] \hat{n}_{iW}, \tag{3}$$

$$\boldsymbol{I}_{\text{following}} = \begin{cases} \hat{n}_{PX_i^t}, \text{if } \boldsymbol{d}_{ij}(t) \geq D_{min}, \\ Decelerate, otherwise. \end{cases} \tag{4}$$

Here, i is the target agent, W and j denote static obstacle and other agent (i.e. other pedestrian or car) respectively, τ denotes a relaxation time, $\boldsymbol{v}^*_i(t)$ and $\boldsymbol{v}_i(t)$ are the desired and current velocities of i respectively. $F_{ij} = \lambda + (1-\lambda)\frac{1+\cos\varphi_{ij}}{2}$ represents an-isotropic behaviour of human, where λ denotes the strength of interactions from behind and φ_{ij} represents the angle between i and j. V_{ij}^o and U_{iW}^o indicate the interaction strengths, σ and R denote the range of these repulsive interactions, $\boldsymbol{d}_{ij}(t)$ and $\boldsymbol{d}_{iW}(t)$ are the distances from i to j and i to W at a specific time, $\hat{n}_{ij}$, $\hat{n}_{iW}$ and $\hat{n}_{PX_i^t}$ denote the normalised vectors. In Eq. (4), $P = \boldsymbol{X}_i^t + \hat{v}_j(t) * D_{min}$, a position behind the leader car and $\boldsymbol{X}_i$ is the current position of i, D_{min} is the minimum car distance, $\hat{v}_j(t)$ denotes the normalised velocity of j. In GSFM, $\boldsymbol{I}_{\text{stopping}}$ happens only if pedestrian(s) have already initiated walking in front to the car, so the car decelerates to let the pedestrian(s) pass.

The game-theoretic module is responsible for handling complex interactions i.e. pedestrian(s)-to-car(s) or car-to-car interaction. A sequential leader-follower game, a.k.a. Stackelberg game is used to handle these interactions. In such a game, both leader and follower players try to maximise their utility: the leader player chooses a strategy first by considering all possible reactions of follower players and the followers react based on the chosen strategy of the leader [31]. Note: the terminology leader and follower have different meanings in car following (e.g., leader: the car in front) and in the Stackelberg game (e.g., leader: the agent whos make decision first). We apply the sub-game perfect Nash equilibrium

(SPNE) to find the optimal strategy pair, denoted by Eq. (5).

$$SPNE = \{s_l \in S_l | max(u_l(s_l, Bs_f(s_l)))\}, \forall s_l \in S_l. \tag{5}$$

$$Bs_f(s_l) = \{s_f \in S_f | max(u_f(s_f | s_l))\}. \tag{6}$$

Eq (6) is the best answer from the follower. Here, s_l, s_f, u_l, u_f and S_l, S_f are the leader's and followers' strategies, utilities regarding the respective strategies and their strategy sets respectively. Each complex interaction is resolved by playing an individual Stackelberg game and the games are not dependent on each other. For any game, the number of leaders is set to one and followers to one or more, and the faster agent (i.e. car) is chosen as the leader. If any complex situation involves more than one cars e.g, pedestrian(s)-to-cars interaction, then the one who detects the

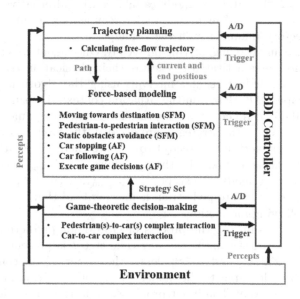

Fig. 1. Trajectory prediction in shared spaces using GSFM. Here, **AF** means added force to classical SFM and **A/D** indicates activation/deactivation of a module in GSFM.

conflict first is set as the leader. To calculate the payoff matrix of the game: firstly, all strategies of the players are ordinarily valued with the assumption that safety and efficiency are their main concerns; secondly, we consider some relevant observable factors to capture courtesy behaviour and situation dynamics, more details about payoff estimation is given in [19,20]. In GSFM, *Continue*, *Decelerate* and *Deviate* (pedestrian only) are the possible strategies for agents.

- Continue: Any pedestrian α crosses vehicle β from the point $P_\alpha = X_\beta^t + F_s * \overrightarrow{e}_\beta$, if $line(X_\alpha^t, E_\alpha)$ intersects $line(X_\beta^t + F_s * \overrightarrow{e}_\beta, X_\beta^t - \frac{F_s}{2} * \overrightarrow{e}_\beta)$, otherwise free-flow movement is continued. Here, $\overrightarrow{e}$ is the direction vector, F_s denotes scaling factor, X^t and E represent current and goal positions respectively. In case of vehicles, they always follow their free-flow movement.
- Decelerate: Road users decelerate and in the end stop (if necessary). For pedestrians, $newSpeed_\alpha = \frac{Speed_\alpha(t)}{2}$ and in case of vehicles, $newSpeed_\beta = Speed_\beta(t) - decRate$.

  Here, $decRate = \begin{cases} \frac{Speed_\beta(t)}{2}, \text{if } distance(\alpha, \beta) \leq D_{min}, \\ \frac{Speed_\beta^2(t)}{distance(\alpha,\beta) - D_{min}}, \text{otherwise.} \end{cases}$

  D_{min} is the critical spatial distance.

– Deviate: A pedestrian α passes a vehicle β from behind from a position $P_\alpha = X_\beta^t - F_s * \overrightarrow{e}_\beta$ (as long as β stays in range of the field of view (FOV) of α) and after that α resumes moving towards its original destination.

Although these modules take control alternatively, at the start of the simulation, GSFM maintains a hierarchy among its modules: it starts with the trajectory planning with the assumption that agents plan their trajectory before starting walking/driving physically. Once agent gets there trajectory, force-based module is activated to execute their physical movement. Conflict recognition is performed at regular intervals using the algorithm proposed in our previous paper [20]. Based on the situation context (i.e. simple or complex conflict), the BDI controller activates either force-based or game module to decide on strategies. Once the strategies are decided, the force-based module is activated again (if not activated already) to execute them. The BDI controller also prioritises the decision taken by these modules, i.e. I_{game} takes precedence over decision of other modules, except for $I_{stopping}$, with the premise that complex interaction e.g. car-to-pedestrian is more critical than pedestrian-to-pedestrian or car following interaction.

To sum up, the process of GSFM for predicting the movement behaviour of any target agent i in any time step t is presented in Eq. (7)–(9). Here, i, j, W, Z_i, X_i^t, and $Y^{t+\Delta t}$ depict the target agent, competitive pedestrian, static obstacle, input to the model, the agent's position in current and next time step respectively. The input profile Z_i is derived from the observation of X_i, which contains start, goal, speed profile of i, and minimum distance acceptance of i with others. The goal of i is estimated by using the heading in the last observed position and average speed over the observed time steps.

$$\text{Pedestrian:}\ \frac{\overrightarrow{dv^t}_i}{dt} = \left(\overrightarrow{D}_i^o + \Sigma \overrightarrow{I}_{iW} + \Sigma \overrightarrow{I}_{ij}\right) or\ \overrightarrow{I}_{game}, \tag{7}$$

$$\text{Car:}\ \frac{\overrightarrow{dv^t}_i}{dt} = \overrightarrow{D}_i^o\ or\ \overrightarrow{I}_{following}\ or\ \overrightarrow{I}_{game}\ or\ \overrightarrow{I}_{stopping}, \tag{8}$$

$$\hat{Y}_i^{t+\Delta t} = f(Z_i, (\frac{\overrightarrow{dv^t}_i}{dt} + X_i^t)). \tag{9}$$

2.3   LSTM with DBSCAN

We pursue a DL model, called Long Short-Term Memories with Density-Based Spatial Clustering of Applications with Noise (LSTM-DBSCAN). For a target agent i, $f(X_i)$ is LSTM-DBSCAN that takes X_i as input and outputs $\hat{Y}_i$. The LSTM-DBSCAN contains two modules: a *mapping module* for interaction pooling and an *LSTM module* for motion planning, see Fig. 2.

The mapping module is used for pooling the interactions between the target agent and other neighbourhood agents at each time step. It follows the idea of repulsive force in SFM [15] to map the collision probability based on safety

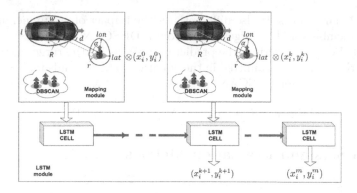

Fig. 2. The structure of LSTM-DBSCAN for target agent i. $\otimes$ stands for the concatenation of the output of the mapping module and the target agent's position at each time step.

distance maintained by the target and neighbourhood agents, denoted by probability density mapping (PDM). Safety distance d (see Fig. 2) is measured from the approximate mass points from the target agent to the neighbourhood agent. If two agents approach each other, PDM increases exponentially. In addition, we follow the same idea as [8] to extend safety distance with buffers for pedestrian personal space [12] and car geometry, denoted by the egg shapes with approximate radius (r or R) in Fig. 2. Radius are extracted from real-world interactions with the differentiation of road users' transport mode.

However, short distance does not necessarily indicate high collision probability. Pedestrians from one group tend to walk at the same speed and maintain a certain distance, to synchronize their speed and distance for communication and visibility between each other [28,32]. Therefore, inside the mapping module, a DBSCAN cluster [10] is incorporated to detect pedestrian groups, so as to cancel out erroneous collision indication and relax on close interactions for group members. At each time step in the observation time, present agents are clustered. The minimum number of points (MinPts) is set to two as the smallest group (cluster) only contains two agents. The maximum Euclidean distance (ϵ) from neighbourhood point to the core points in a DBSCAN cluster is set to one meter. A neighbourhood agent is defined as a group member for the target agent if they co-exist in the same cluster over 90% of the observed time steps. Both ϵ and the overlap ratio of time steps are decided from the hyper-parameter searching in [6]. During clustering, PDM is reset to zero for group members.

The LSTM module is used for motion planning, which takes the target agent's coordinates and the interactions with neighbourhood agents using PDM as input at each observed time step. In prediction time, similar to Social-LSTM [2], the LSTM module uses the encoded information from observed time steps to predict the distribution of the next positions. While, our DL model differs from Social-LSTM by semantically quantifying all the neighbourhood agents' impact using a collision probability, instead of occupancy grid within a predefined interactive zone using binary values. It also differentiates the impact of group members and non-group members on the target agent from a DBSCAN cluster.

In short, Eq. (10) describes the prediction process for the target agent i. For simplicity, the time step is omitted in the equation. $f(.,.)$ stands for LSTM, $\phi(.)$ for PDM, and $\psi(.,.)$ for DBSCAN.

$$\hat{Y}_{i \in N} = f(X_{i \in N}, \phi(\psi(X_{i \in N}, X_{j \in N, j \neq i}))) \tag{10}$$

3   Data Sets and Evaluation Metrics

3.1   Data Sets

To evaluate the performance of the proposed two models, we use two data sets with mixed traffic trajectories extracted from shared spaces of different layout (Fig. 3), namely, the Hamburg Bergedorf station data set (HBS) from Germany [26] and the DUT data set from the campus of Dalian University of Technology in China [33]. The layout of HBS is a street with pedestrian crossing from both sides. The DUT data set has 11 clips recorded in a roundabout and 17 clips recorded in an intersection. The clip from HBS contains dynamic pedestrians-to-vehicles interactions. Whereas, the clips from DUT have less vehicles, but more vehicles-to-crowd interactions [33]. Table 1 summarises the statistics for each data set. The first 1200 time steps of the HBS data set and 12 clips (8 from the intersection and 4 from the roundabout) from the DUT data set are used for extracting interaction scenarios for evaluation. In total, we manually extracted 89 scenarios that involve interactions between pedestrians and vehicles: 67 scenarios from HBS and 22 from DUT. Please note that due to the short length of clips from DUT, scenarios extracted from DUT are shorter than the ones from HBS. The rest of the two data sets are used for calibrating the expert-based model GSFM and training the DL model LSTM-DBSCAN. There is no overlap between the evaluation and training data.

Table 1. Statistics for each data set

Data set	#Time steps	Time-step duration	#Ped	#Veh	Layout description
HBS	3620	0.5 s	1115	338	1 clip in a street
DUT	648	0.5 s	1767	69	11 clips in a roundabout 17 clips in an intersection

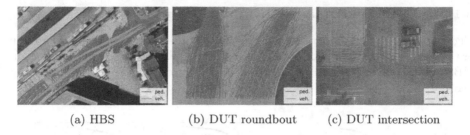

| (a) HBS | (b) DUT roundbout | (c) DUT intersection |

Fig. 3. Mixed trajectories from shared spaces of different layout

3.2 Evaluation Metrics

To evaluate the performance of GSFM and LSTM-BDSCAN in terms of realistic trajectory prediction, i.e. to minimise the difference from the ground-truth trajectories by considering both accident/conflict-avoidance and behaviour modelling, we use displacement (Euclidean and Hausdorff distance) and heading errors as metrics. As commonly used in other works [2,13], the average Euclidean distance error (ADE) measures the aligned error for each step and we report the value averaged over the paths. For the accumulated error, we use Hausdorff distance to measure the largest distance from the set of the predicted positions of a trajectory to the set of true positions [24]. In most cases, the displacement error accumulates with the increment of time steps. The Hausdorff distance error is very similar to the displacement error for the final position. Heading (from the previous position to the next position) error measures the pairwise absolute heading difference over all positions between the predicted and ground truth trajectories.

Due to the stochastic characteristics of human movement behaviour, different road users may behave in different ways in a given situation [21]. In this regard, it is very difficult to quantify which way of behaving is better than the other. The quantitative evaluation metrics alone may not be sufficient to demonstrate the feasibility of a trajectory prediction model. Therefore, we perform case studies to analyse how both proposed models handle different real-world scenarios.

4 Experimental Results

GSFM is implemented using a BDI multi-agent framework, LightJason [3]. LSTM-DBSCAN is implemented using tensorflow [1] framework. The LSTM units have a size of 128 and one vertical layer. It is trained using RMSProp optimised with a learning rate of 0.003 and batch size of 16 for 300 epochs. The observation sequence length is set to six time steps and the prediction sequence length varies with a minimum length of six time steps. Both GSFM and LSTM-DBSCAN are tested on real-world scenarios lasting different length of time steps, unlike [2,13,29] that predict trajectories of a fixed length of time steps.

4.1   Quantitative Results for Individual Models

Figure 4 shows the comparison among the ground-truth trajectories and the trajectory predictions by LSTM-DBSCAN and GSFM along time horizon on HBS and DUT, measured by Euclidean and Hausdorff distance, and heading error.

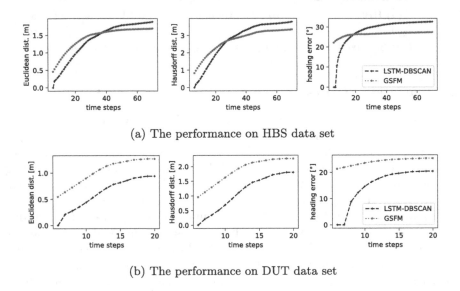

(a) The performance on HBS data set

(b) The performance on DUT data set

Fig. 4. The performance of GSFM and GSFM-w-LSTM on different data sets.

In general, as the time step increases, the performance of both models decreases on both data sets, as the uncertainty increases further into the future. Figure 4a shows that LSTM-DBSCAN performs better in short-sequence prediction (approximately 25 time-steps) than GSFM by all measurements for the HBS data set, which contains many long-sequence interactions. However, the performance of LSTM-DBSCAN degrades faster than GSFM with the increasing time steps.

From Fig. 4b, the performance for LSTM-DBSCAN on DUT is significantly better than GSFM regarding all the evaluation metrics. As mentioned before (see Sect. 3.1), the scenarios from DUT are shorter and more complicated due to the high density of traffic in the intersection and the roundabout than HBS. Both of the proposed models have a limited capacity to deal with dense traffic.

4.2   Qualitative Results for Individual Models

Figure 5 shows the predictions made by GSFM and LSTM-DBSCAN in different scenarios. In most scenarios denoted in the sub-figures, both GSFM and LSTM-DBSCAN generate feasible trajectories in interactions within a small number of

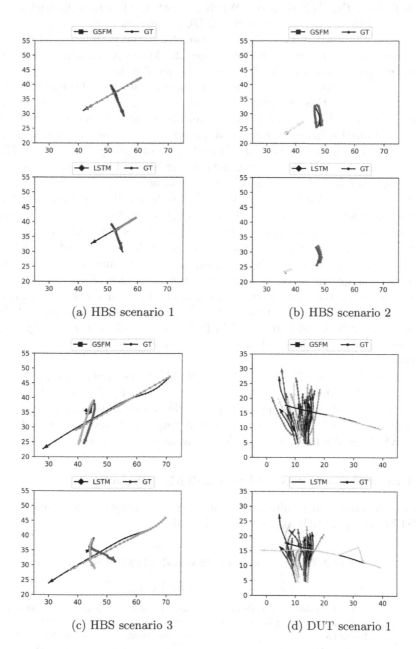

(a) HBS scenario 1   (b) HBS scenario 2

(c) HBS scenario 3   (d) DUT scenario 1

Fig. 5. Comparison of the predictions by GSFM and LSTM-DBSCAN. Ground-truth trajectories are in black colour and predicted trajectories are colour-coded. Vehicles are travelling in either diagonal or slightly horizontal directions. The arrows indicate the moving directions of pedestrians and vehicles.

road users from the HBS data set. Whereas, both models have limited performance in dealing with dense traffic in the DUT data set.

Based on the visualisation, the prediction from the GSFM model overlaps the ground truth well and outperforms the LSTM-DBSCAN model when the trajectories have a constant heading direction (see Fig. 5a).

However, when road users change their heading direction, GSFM may have difficulty mimicking this behaviour. As can be seen in Fig. 5b, the trajectories generated by GSFM are straight forward and homogeneous as the model only specifies a limited number of behaviour patterns based on the assumption of relatively fixed speed (i.e. a Gaussian distribution of speed). Else-ways, LSTM-DBSCAN can automatically capture both the speed and orientation attributes of each road user based on a short observation time.

Moreover, GSFM and LSTM-DBSCAN handle conflicts differently. GSFM deals with conflicts explicitly either based on the social forces, where the repulsive force increases exponentially when two road users come closer [15] or by game playing to negotiate on the priority over road spaces. In contrast, LSTM-DBSCAN learns collision avoidance based on the training data with probability density mapping automatically. They may generate different negotiating results even facing the same interactions. For example, in Fig. 5c, both GSFM and LSTM-DBSCAN predict that both pedestrians crossing the street before the upcoming vehicle, although LSTM-DBSCAN predicts a more aggressive behaviour for the vehicle which results in a near collision with the crossing pedestrians.

In Fig. 5d, both GSFM and LSTM-DBSCAN do not optimally predict the trajectory for the vehicle approaching a large number of pedestrians. In GSFM, the vehicle decelerates and some of the pedestrians accelerate for collision avoidance. Whereas, LSTM-DBSCAN generates a very unfeasible trajectory for the vehicle, which results in pedestrians deviating from the upcoming vehicle.

4.3   Pros and Cons of GSFM and LSTM-DBSCAN

Based on the empirical results, we summarise the strengths and weaknesses of the GSFM and LSTM-DBSCAN models in Table 2.

Table 2. Pros and cons of GSFM and LSTM-DBSCAN

Model	GSFM	LSTM-DBSCAN
Pros	Transparent, explainable, collision-free trajectories, no need for labelled data, easy to control	Less domain knowledge, not based on rules, good short-term predictions, realistic predictions in simple scenarios
Cons	Domain knowledge, complicated rules, homogeneous predictions, inflexible in scaled problems, limited in dense traffic	Not transparent, not explainable, collision-free trajectories not guaranteed, computationally inefficient, might be over-fitted, limited in dense traffic, require labelled data, hard to control

Some pioneer studies [16,27] indicate that a hybrid model can be used to hoard the collective advantages of both kinds of approaches. Therefore, in future, we consider to combine the expert-based and DL approaches to model collision-free, explainable, and heterogeneous trajectories of agents.

5   Conclusion and Future Work

In this study, we propose an expert-based model and a deep learning model for mixed traffic trajectory modelling and prediction in shared spaces of different layout. Both of the two models take the same input data for a fair comparison. Their performance is evaluated on real-world shared-space scenarios, such as interactions between pedestrians and vehicles. In most cases, both models can predict realistic trajectories for mixed traffic agents. The expert-based model, using Social Force Model and Game theory, predicts collision-free trajectories. While the predictions tend to be homogeneous. The deep learning model that manipulates Long Short-Term Memories and density clustering predicts accurate short-term trajectories. However, its performance decreases significantly for longer-term prediction and it may generate (near) collision predictions. Both models have limited performance in coping with a large number of agents.

To improve the performance and robustness of the individual models, more open-source data sets of shared spaces will be used for training and evaluation. We can build a hybrid model by combining the collision-avoidance mechanism of the expert model with the motion planning techniques of the DL model [18], to predict collision-free and realistic trajectories in mixed traffic environments.

References

1. Abadi, M., Agarwal, A., Barham, P., et al.: TensorFlow: large-scale machine learning on heterogeneous systems (2015). Software available from tensorflow.org. http://tensorflow.org/
2. Alahi, A., Goel, K., Ramanathan, V., Robicquet, A., Fei-Fei, L., Savarese, S.: Social LSTM: human trajectory prediction in crowded spaces. In: Proceedings of the IEEE Conference on Computer Vision and Pattern Recognition, pp. 961–971 (2016)
3. Aschermann, M., Kraus, P., Müller, J.P.: LightJason. In: Criado Pacheco, N., Carrascosa, C., Osman, N., Julián Inglada, V. (eds.) EUMAS/AT -2016. LNCS (LNAI), vol. 10207, pp. 58–66. Springer, Cham (2017). https://doi.org/10.1007/978-3-319-59294-7_6
4. Bandini, S., Crociani, L., Vizzari, G.: An approach for managing heterogeneous speed profiles in cellular automata pedestrian models. J. Cell. Autom. **12**(5), 401–421 (2017)
5. Bjørnskau, T.: The zebra crossing game-using game theory to explain a discrepancy between road user behaviour and traffic rules. Saf. Sci. **92**, 298–301 (2017)
6. Cheng, H., Li, Y., Sester, M.: Pedestrian group detection in shared space. In: 2019 IEEE Intelligent Vehicles Symposium (IV), pp. 1707–1714. IEEE (2019)

7. Cheng, H., Sester, M.: Mixed traffic trajectory prediction using LSTM–based models in shared space. In: Mansourian, A., Pilesjö, P., Harrie, L., van Lammeren, R. (eds.) AGILE 2018. LNGC, pp. 309–325. Springer, Cham (2018). https://doi.org/10.1007/978-3-319-78208-9_16

8. Cheng, H., Sester, M.: Modeling mixed traffic in shared space using LSTM with probability density mapping. In: 2018 21st International Conference on Intelligent Transportation Systems (ITSC), pp. 3898–3904. IEEE (2018)

9. Clarke, E.: Shared space: the alternative approach to calming traffic. Traffic Eng. Control **47**(8), 290–292 (2006)

10. Ester, M., Kriegel, H.P., Sander, J., Xu, X., et al.: A density-based algorithm for discovering clusters in large spatial databases with noise. In: KDD 1996, pp. 226–231 (1996)

11. Franke, U., Gavrila, D., Görzig, S., Lindner, F., Paetzold, F., Wöhler, C.: Autonomous driving goes downtown. Intell. Syst. **13**(6), 40–48 (1998)

12. Gérin-Lajoie, M., Richards, C.L., McFadyen, B.J.: The negotiation of stationary and moving obstructions during walking: anticipatory locomotor adaptations and preservation of personal space. Mot. Control **9**(3), 242–269 (2005)

13. Gupta, A., Johnson, J., Fei-Fei, L., Savarese, S., Alahi, A.: Social GAN: socially acceptable trajectories with generative adversarial networks. In: Proceedings of the IEEE Conference on Computer Vision and Pattern Recognition, pp. 2255–2264 (2018)

14. Hamilton-Baillie, B.: Shared space: reconciling people, places and traffic. Built Environ. **34**(2), 161–181 (2008)

15. Helbing, D., Molnar, P.: Social force model for pedestrian dynamics. Phys. Rev. E **51**(5), 4282 (1995)

16. Hu, Z., Ma, X., Liu, Z., Hovy, E., Xing, E.: Harnessing deep neural networks with logic rules. arXiv preprint arXiv:1603.06318 (2016)

17. Ivanovic, B., Schmerling, E., Leung, K., Pavone, M.: Generative modeling of multimodal multi-human behavior. arXiv preprint arXiv:1803.02015 (2018)

18. Johora, F.T., Cheng, H., Müller, J.P., Sester, M.: An agent-based model for trajectory modelling in shared spaces: a combination of expert-based and deep learning approaches. In: Proceedings of the 19th International Conference on Autonomous Agents and MultiAgent Systems, pp. 1878–1880 (2020)

19. Johora, F.T., Müller, J.P.: Modeling interactions of multimodal road users in shared spaces. In: 2018 21st International Conference on Intelligent Transportation Systems (ITSC), pp. 3568–3574. IEEE (2018)

20. Johora, F.T., Müller, J.P.: Zone-specific interaction modeling of pedestrians and cars in shared spaces. Transp. Res. Procedia **47**, 251–258 (2020)

21. Kaparias, I., Bell, M.G., Miri, A., Chan, C., Mount, B.: Analysing the perceptions of pedestrians and drivers to shared space. Transp. Res. Part F Traffic Psychol. Behav. **15**(3), 297–310 (2012)

22. LeCun, Y., Bengio, Y., Hinton, G.: Deep learning. Nature **521**(7553), 436 (2015)

23. Lee, N., Choi, W., Vernaza, P., Choy, C.B., Torr, P.H., Chandraker, M.: DESIRE: distant future prediction in dynamic scenes with interacting agents. In: Proceedings of the IEEE Conference on Computer Vision and Pattern Recognition, pp. 336–345 (2017)

24. Munkres, J.R.: Topology. Prentice Hall, Upper Saddle River (2000)

25. Nagel, K., Schreckenberg, M.: A cellular automaton model for freeway traffic. J. Phys. I **2**(12), 2221–2229 (1992)

26. Pascucci, F., Rinke, N., Schiermeyer, C., Berkhahn, V., Friedrich, B.: A discrete choice model for solving conflict situations between pedestrians and vehicles in shared space. arXiv preprint arXiv:1709.09412 (2017)
27. Pedreschi, D., Giannotti, F., Guidotti, R., Monreale, A., Ruggieri, S., Turini, F.: Meaningful explanations of black box AI decision systems. In: Proceedings of the AAAI Conference on Artificial Intelligence, vol. 33, pp. 9780–9784 (2019)
28. Rinke, N., Schiermeyer, C., Pascucci, F., Berkhahn, V., Friedrich, B.: A multi-layer social force approach to model interactions in shared spaces using collision prediction. Transp. Res. Procedia **25**, 1249–1267 (2017)
29. Sadeghian, A., Kosaraju, V., Sadeghian, A., Hirose, N., Savarese, S.: SoPhie: an attentive GAN for predicting paths compliant to social and physical constraints. arXiv preprint arXiv:1806.01482 (2018)
30. Schmidhuber, J.: Deep learning in neural networks: an overview. Neural Netw. **61**, 85–117 (2015)
31. Schönauer, R.: A microscopic traffic flow model for shared space. Ph.D. thesis, Graz University of Technology (2017)
32. Yamaguchi, K., Berg, A.C., Ortiz, L.E., Berg, T.L.: Who are you with and where are you going? In: 2011 IEEE Conference on Computer Vision and Pattern Recognition (CVPR), pp. 1345–1352. IEEE (2011)
33. Yang, D., Li, L., Redmill, K., Özgüner, Ü.: Top-view trajectories: a pedestrian dataset of vehicle-crowd interaction from controlled experiments and crowded campus. arXiv preprint arXiv:1902.00487 (2019)
34. Yang, D., Özgüner, Ü., Redmill, K.: Social force based microscopic modeling of vehicle-crowd interaction. In: 2018 IEEE Intelligent Vehicles Symposium (IV), pp. 1537–1542. IEEE (2018)

Towards Agent-Based Traffic Simulation Using Live Data from Sensors for Smart Cities

Yan Qian⬛, Johan Barthelemy$^{(\boxtimes)}$⬛, and Pascal Perez⬛

SMART Infrastructure Facility, University of Wollongong,
Wollongong, NSW, Australia
{yq978,johan,pascal}@uow.edu.au
https://www.uow.edu.au/smart

Abstract. The Smart City and Internet-of-Things revolutions enable the collection of various types of data in real-time through sensors. This data can be used to improve the decision tools and simulations used by city planners. This paper presents a new framework for real-time traffic simulation integrating an agent-based methodology with live CCTV and other sensor data while respecting the privacy regulations. The framework simulates traffic flows of pedestrians, vehicles and bicycles and their interactions. The approach has been applied in Liverpool (NSW, Australia) showing promising preliminary results and can easily ingest additional sensor data, e.g. air quality.

Keywords: Traffic simulation · Agent-based modelling · Data-driven simulation · Edge computing · Smart city · Intelligent video analytics

1 Introduction

With massive increases in the world's population and nearly 70% of the world population projected to live in urban areas by 2050, cities face serious urban planning challenges [1]. Not only do they face rapidly growing population, but they also have to deal with social and sustainability challenges. To better cope with changes, cities need long-term approaches leading to sustainability [2].

Rethinking cities to not only efficiently manage their current situation and population, but also their future growth is exactly the main motivation behind the concept of smart cities. While there is no consensual definition of what a smart city is [3], it commonly involves the usage of Information and Communication Technologies (ICT) to design tools which should respond to people's needs through sustainable solutions for social and economic challenges.

S. Swarup and B. T. R. Savarimuthu (Eds.): MABS 2020, LNAI 12316, pp. 28–40, 2021.
https://doi.org/10.1007/978-3-030-66888-4_3

Bibri and Krogstie [4,5] proposed an interdisciplinary literature review of smart and sustainable cities and pointed out the interest of a new generation of urban planning tools for improving mobility and accessibility. A smart city is then a significant tool for municipalities which can reduce their spending and perform real-time monitoring of their transportation, energy and utilities networks [6]. These planning tools require a large amount of data that can be nowadays collected via different type of sensors and devices deployed within the city.

Currently, many cities around the world are rapidly developing their existing CCTV network. These large surveillance networks represent a major cost for the councils in terms of maintenance, but are only used for investigating incidents and monitoring anti-social behaviours in public places [7]. This is due to stringent privacy regulations, as only the police and a few accredited operators are allowed to view the live or recorded video feeds. This results in the expensive collection of a vast amount of rich data that have been mostly unused so far.

This paper presents a new framework for real-time traffic simulation integrating an agent-based methodology with existing CCTV data, effectively addressing the issues of the surveillance camera maintenance cost by adding new usages while respecting the privacy regulations.

The paper is organized as follows. Section 2 introduces the challenges of obtaining traffic counts. Section 3 describes the Liverpool Smart Pedestrian project monitoring mobility and air quality within the Australian city of Liverpool. Section 4 then details the visual sensor used to capture the traffic flows within the city. Section 5 describes the use of the collected data within an agent-based traffic simulation. This is followed in Sect. 6 by preliminary results of the approach applied in Liverpool. Concluding remarks and perspective are presented in the last section.

2   Collecting Traffic Counts

The first stage for monitoring and modelling traffic in a road network is collecting traffic counts. Inductive loop detectors, pneumatic road tubes, and temporary manual counts have been the primary methods for collecting such traffic data. The development of automatic sensing technologies, to replace manual counting, has allowed a higher frequency rate as well as the permanent monitoring of the traffic counts [8]. Other classic traffic counter devices include piezo-electric sensors and radar-based off-roads sensors [9,10]. While initially being designed for vehicular traffic, most of them can also be adapted to count bicycles and pedestrians [11].

With the drastic reduction in the cost of electronic components, and recent advances in machine learning and image processing, it is now possible to develop at relatively low cost, edge computing solutions to monitor traffic. For example, Gupta et al. [12] designed low-cost hardware using Wi-Fi strength as a signal to monitor traffic. The passage of a car between a transmitter and a receiver produces a variation in signal strength that can be measured to count vehicles flows. However, this approach still needs new infrastructures. Another approach is to rely on already existing infrastructures to perform real-time monitoring. Indeed, as cities have been massively investing in CCTV networks [13], retrofitting the already existing CCTV infrastructure to transform classical CCTV into smart CCTV becomes a promising approach to real-time monitoring of traffic. Consequently, more and more research is being done using video analytics on CCTV footage. For example, Kim et al. [14] used CCTV in an urban traffic information system to determine traffic speed and volume, and combine this information with on-board wireless equipment to estimate travel speed.

Finally, when using CCTV footage, ensuring privacy is a major issue. As noted by Satyanarayanan et al. [15,16] and Shi et al. [17,18], the edge computing paradigm offers a way to process data at the edge of the network to address concerns such as bandwidth saving, as well as data safety and privacy. Indeed, the privacy of the data is ensured by the processing which denatures the raw data [19]. The resulting transmitted data has typically a significantly smaller size than the original raw data as it contains only the relevant information for the application.

The design of an edge computing device with the ability to perform real-time analysis of CCTV would then allow not only to collect data but also to ensure privacy as the image feeds would not leave the already existing CCTV network and only denatured data would be produced by the device. This is the approach retained in the project briefly introduced in the next section.

3   The Liverpool Smart Pedestrians Project

The Liverpool Smart Pedestrians project was funded under the Australian Government Smart Cities and Suburbs Program for a duration of one year starting from February 2018. It was a collaboration between the Liverpool City Council and the University of Wollongong. The project aimed to design innovative solutions for the collection of data in a non-intrusive way to help inform urban planning in Liverpool, a suburb of Sydney in New South Wales, Australia [19].

The city is growing rapidly, with more housing, offices and educational facilities. The council's redevelopment of its CBD is expected to bring in 30,000 additional pedestrians per day. All of this makes the city a good area for experiments monitoring the effect of this redevelopment on the traffic.

The results of workshops conducted with the community and the feedback from the city urban planners highlighted the need for sensors monitoring the traffic with the following requirements:

– *Multi-modal detection and tracking*: The sensors need to be able to detect and track pedestrians, vehicles and cyclists.
– *Privacy compliant*: As sensors are going to be deployed over a city, the sensors should be privacy compliant, meaning that no personal data should be stored or exchanged. Since no raw image will be saved by the device, nor transmitted to a centralised server, there are no privacy issues.
– *Leveraging existing infrastructures*: As cities already make huge investments on CCTV systems [13], the solution should take advantage of the already existing infrastructures in terms of networks and cameras. Retrofitting the existing CCTV network to collect more data has been identified as a major innovation.
– *Scalability and interoperability*: New sensors can be added at any time, regardless their technologies, meaning the sensor network can be easily expanded and capture new type of data.

Thus, the project aims were to develop and evaluate mobility trackers using CCTV live feeds. Twenty visual sensors have been deployed over the city centre to monitor traffic flows. Fifteen of them use already existing CCTVs while five of them are new mobile CCTV units allowing relocation if needed.

These new visual sensors are capable of tracking and automatically differentiating various types of traffic components such as cars, buses, bicycles or pedestrians in real-time. The processed data is then transmitted to a centralized database and can be visualized on a dashboard in real-time or used to develop an agent-based simulation to infer in real-time the dynamics of the traffic flows in the road network.

As part of this pilot project, 20 air quality and noise sensors are also co-located with the mobility trackers to evaluate the impact of the traffic on air quality and noise pollution. Figure 1 displays a map of the town centre and the location of the sensors.

4 An Edge Computing Device for Traffic Monitoring

The objective of the project was to deploy a fleet of these sensors enabling city-wide traffic monitoring in real-time. For that purpose of monitoring the mobility within a network, we have designed a sensor that is able to detect and track entities of interest in a live video feed using intelligent video analytics. The most important feature of the sensor is that it follows the edge computing paradigm, i.e., the video analytics are run directly on the device and only the results of the processing are transmitted. This has two main advantages:

– It lowers the network bandwidth requirement as no raw images are transmitted, but only indicators and meta-data; and
– Thanks to the limited amount of information being transmitted, the device is privacy compliant.

The privacy compliance of the device is critical for real world applications and deployment in smart cities. Indeed, the system can be paired with existing CCTV infrastructure while not transmitting the actual video feed captured from the cameras. This lowers the deployment cost of the sensor as no additional camera is needed while allowing uses of the already existing CCTV infrastructure.

The sensor performs the following steps iteratively on average 20 times each second:

1. Frame acquisition;
2. Detecting the entities of interests in the current frame via YOLOv3 [20];

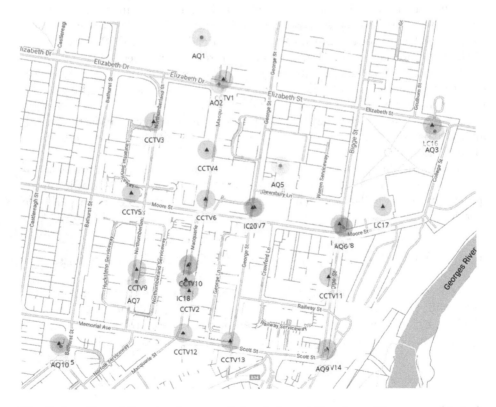

Fig. 1. Location of the visual sensors (triangles), and the air quality sensors (circles) in Liverpool.

3. Tracking by matching the current detections with the ones in the previous frame via the SORT algorithm [21];
4. Updating the trajectories of entities already stored in the device database or creating records for the newly detected objects.

In parallel, the device regularly transmits the outputs, i.e. the trajectories and number of entities tracked, either over Ethernet or LoRaWAN networks, the latter being a wireless long range, low power network well suited for the Internet of Things. The interested reader can find a complete description of the visual sensor in [19].

5 Using Live Data in Traffic Simulation

The proposed model receives in real-time data from the sensors which is used to generate origin-destination matrices to estimate the demand on the network. The origins and destinations correspond to the sensors' locations in the network which will be thus acting as generator of travelling agents and attractor for those agents. A newly generated agent will then compute a path to a randomly selected destination. The random draw is weighted against the traffic count observed by the sensors. It should be noted that a travelling agent can represent either a pedestrian, a bicycle or a vehicle as the smart visual sensor is able to detect and differentiate those three types of entities.

The class diagram of the model, Fig. 2, shows the interaction between the different agents. Note that the air quality sensors and CCTV sensors are not merged into a single class, as they do not share the same attributes. Like Rodrique et al. [22] we make the difference between fixed agents, in the sense that they do not affect the movements during the simulation, and travelling agents:

– Fixed agents:

- **CCTV Sensor**: They represent the smart visual sensors in Liverpool. The travelling agents are created and removed at the sensors' locations.
- **Air Quality Sensor**: They represent the air quality sensors in Liverpool. The travelling agents are assigned pollution exposure based on those sensors.
- **Traffic Signal**: They represent the traffic lights in the road network. The travelling agents stop at the traffic signals depending on their colour. If the frequency of traffic light changes is known, the simulation is able to predict the roads chosen by the travelling agents (pedestrians/vehicles).

- **Road**: The roads of the road network on which the travelling agents move. Note that in the model, a difference between the roads for pedestrians and the roads for vehicles is made, as some roads are only accessible for pedestrians and not for vehicles. In our class diagram, we merge both roads (roads for vehicles and roads for pedestrians) into one agent *road*, as they share the same attributes, e.g. direction, name, length, etc.

- Travelling agents: These agents travel between CCTV sensors and include:

- **Vehicle**: These agents move along the roads at a certain speed.
- **Pedestrian**: These agents represent the pedestrians walking within the network.
- **Bicycle**: These agents illustrate the bicycles.

For simplification purposes, the three different moving entities are merged into one agent *TravellingAgent* in the class diagram (Fig. 2). Finally, the conceptual model drawn for the multi-agents simulation is illustrated in Fig. 3. Figure 4 depicts the creation of the travelling agents using the following steps:

- When the time in the simulation t_{simu} equals to the time of our data t_{start}, our simulation compares the number of travelling agents (pedestrian/vehicle) seen in the simulation ($\#TS$) to the number of travelling agents seen by our smart visual sensors ($\#TR$). If more travelling agents are seen in our data than in our simulation, i.e. $\#TR > \#TS$, then create the number of missing agents in our simulation. If, on the other hand, our simulation sees more agents than our sensors, i.e. $\#TS > \#TR$, then remove that exceeding number of agents from the simulation (as it would mean that less travelling agents were recorded by the sensors). For each travelling agent created at the different sensors, a destination (corresponding to a sensor) is randomly created.
- As we increment a line in our data, we also increment the time, and the travelling agents move on their path (the distance of their movement d will depend on their speed v using $d = v \times t$).
- If the travelling agent's location in the simulation (x_{TS_n}, y_{TS_n}) corresponds to its destination (x_D, y_D), i.e. the agent has arrived to its destination, then remove the travelling agent from the simulation.
- End the simulation if all the data has been read.

The implementation relies on the GAMA platform[1], a free and open agent-based framework with a strong focus on spatial simulations.

---

[1] https://gama-platform.github.io/.

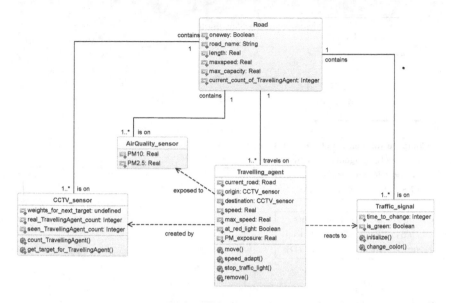

Fig. 2. Model class diagram

6 Preliminary Results

Using the data collected from the smart sensors[2] and the zone data obtained through OpenStreetMap[3], we construct a model simulating the traffic flow in the city of Liverpool in real-time. This model allows us to infer the interactions between the different type travelling agents (pedestrians, cyclists, vehicles) and the fixed agents (sensors), as illustrated in Fig. 5.

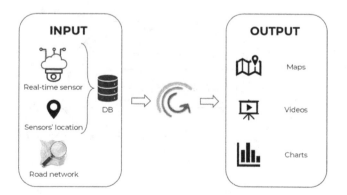

Fig. 3. Design model of the proposed traffic simulation.

---

[2] available at https://pavo.its.uow.edu.au.
[3] https://www.openstreetmap.org/.

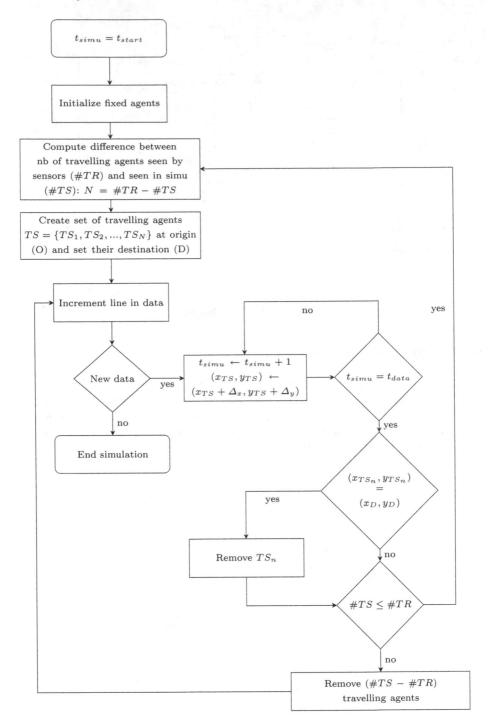

Fig. 4. Activity flowchart. Used notations: t_{simu} is the time in the simulation, whereas t_{start} and t_{data} are the times in the data. (x_{TS_n}, y_{TS_n}) represent the location of the travelling agent at t_{simu}, and (x_D, y_D) the coordinates of its destination.

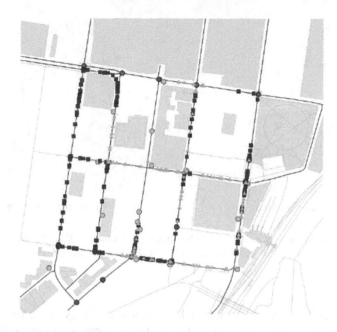

Fig. 5. Traffic network: the red and green circles depict the traffic lights, whereas the blue circles represent the visual sensors. The blue squares represent the vehicles, the yellow triangles illustrate the pedestrians. The date and time of the simulation captured in this picture is 9/11/2019 at 3.02PM.

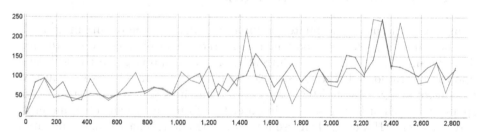

Fig. 6. Traffic flow: number of pedestrians detected by the visual sensors (green) vs number of pedestrians *seen* by the sensors in the simulation (red) per second (Color figure online).

Furthermore, behaviours such as congested roads at certain peak times, points of interests of the road network, exposure of the travelling agents to pollutants, and the evolution of the number of travelling agents in the traffic flow, can be inferred. This is illustrated in Fig. 6.

As it is driven by the data coming from sensors, the proposed model is able to simulate the traffic flows of Liverpool at the macro-level (i.e. at the level of the sensors) and can thus be used to monitor and predict different behaviours of the traffic flows, while respecting the privacy of the citizens.

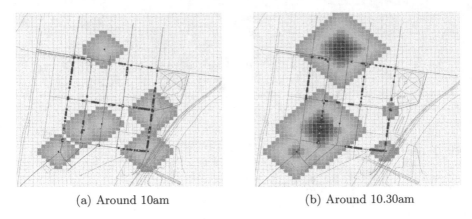

(a) Around 10am   (b) Around 10.30am

Fig. 7. Exposure of the travelling agents to particulate matter (PM) 2.5 on 10/11/2019. The redder (or greener) the color of the cell, the higher (or lower) the PM 2.5 rate is (Color figure online).

As mentioned earlier, air quality sensors are also deployed within Liverpool. It thus possible to use their data and Air Quality agents to determine the air pollution exposure of the travelling agents. This is illustrated in Fig. 7.

7   Conclusion and Future Work

Being able to accurately estimate and forecast traffic flows across urban networks has become crucial for transport managers and urban planners to create more liveable and caring cities [23]. Currently, traffic monitoring mostly still relies upon inductive loop detectors associated with SCATS, an adaptive urban traffic control system adopted by many Australian cities [24]. These detectors are sparsely located at key crossroads in order to inform the syncing of traffic lights across the city. However, their use for proper traffic estimation and simulation is limited and often must be complemented by other means, including manual surveys.

In this work, we are using a new sensor performing real-time traffic monitoring using existing CCTVs, while respecting the privacy regulations. The live data collected from the sensors is then used in an agent-based simulation model to infer the traffic dynamics in real-time. This method can be easily extended to include other types of sensors and data, such as air quality and noise pollution.

The proposed approach does not only deliver a novel approach to accurately monitor and predict different type traffic flows, their interactions and the resulting pollution in cities, but has the potential to be applicable to many other situations where the structure of the network and some partial and local information is known, but the global dynamics are still unknown.

Further work includes taking into consideration the weather data in order to refine the model of the distribution of the air pollutants measured by the air quality sensors [22], establishing a live connection to the data, using more realistic traffic light frequencies, as well as improving the current traffic model by using strategic agents [23] and a state-of-the-art car following model [25].

References

1. United Nations Department of Economic and Social Affairs, "2018 revision of world urbanization prospects" (2018). https://www.un.org/development/desa/en/news/population/2018-revision-of-world-urbanization-prospects.html. Accessed 02 Feb 2020
2. Bulkeley, H., Betsill, M.: Rethinking sustainable cities: multilevel governance and the 'Urban' politics of climate change. Environ. Polit. **14**(1), 42–63 (2005)
3. Albino, V., Berardi, U., Dangelico, R.M.: Smart cities: definitions, dimensions, performance, and initiatives. J. Urban Technol. **22**(1), 3–21 (2015)
4. Bibri, S.E., Krogstie, J.: Smart sustainable cities of the future: an extensive interdisciplinary literature review. Sustain. Cities Soc. **31**, 183–212 (2017)
5. Bibri, S.E., Krogstie, J.: On the social shaping dimensions of smart sustainable cities: a study in science, technology, and society. Sustain. Cities Soc. **29**, 219–246 (2017)
6. Anthopoulos, L.: Smart utopia VS smart reality: learning by experience from 10 smart city cases. Cities **63**, 128–148 (2017)
7. Wilson, D., Sutton, A.: Open-street CCTV in Australia. Australian Institute of Criminology Canberra, Canberra (2003)
8. Commenges, H.: L'invention de la mobilité quotidienne. Aspects performatifs des instruments de la socio-économie des transports. Université Paris-Diderot - Paris VII, Paris, France (2013)
9. Zwahlen, H.T., Russ, A., Oner, E., Parthasarathy, M.: Evaluation of microwave radar trailers for nonintrusive traffic measurements. Trans. Res. Rec. **1917**(1), 124–140 (2005)
10. Middleton, D., Parker, R. T., Longmire, R.: Investigation of Vehicle Detector Performance and ATMS Interface. Texas Transportation Institute, Texas A & M University: College Station, TX, USA (2007)
11. Ryus, P., et al.: Methods and Technologies for Pedestrian and Bicycle Volume Data Collection. Transportation Research Board, Washington, DC (2014)
12. Gupta, S., Hamzin, A., Degbelo, A.: A low-cost open hardware system for collecting traffic data using WI-FI signal strength. Sensors **76**, 159–162 (2018)
13. Lawson, T., Rogerson, R., Barnacle, M.: A comparison between the cost effectiveness of CCTV and improved street lighting as a means of crime reduction. Comput. Environ. Urban Syst. **68**, 17–25 (2018)
14. Kim, T.-H., Ramos, C., Mohammed, S.: Smart city and IoT. Future Gen. Comput. Syst. **76**, 159–162 (2017)
15. Satyanarayanan, M., et al.: Edge analytics in the Internet of Things. IEEE Pervasive Comput. **14**(2), 24–31 (2015)
16. Satyanarayanan, M.: The emergence of edge computing. Computer **50**(1), 30–39 (2017)
17. Shi, W., Dustdar, S.: The promise of edge computing. Computer **49**(5), 78–81 (2016)
18. Shi, W., Cao, J., Zhang, Q., Li, Y., Xu, L.: Edge computing: vision and challenges. IEEE Internet Things J. **3**(5), 637–646 (2016)

19. Barthélemy, J., Verstaevel, N., Forehead, H., Perez, P.: Edge-computing video analytics for real-time traffic monitoring in a smart city. Sensors **19**(9), 2048 (2019)
20. Redmon, J., Farhad, A.: YOLOv3: An Incremental Improvement. arXiv (2018)
21. Bewley, A., Ge, Z., Ott, L., Ramos, F., Upcrof, B.: Simple online and realtime tracking. In: Proceedings of the 2016 IEEE International Conference on Image Processing (ICIP), Phoenix, AZ, USA (2016)
22. Rodrique, K., Ho, T.V., Nguyen, M.H.: An agent-based simulation for studying air pollution from traffic in urban areas: the case of Hanoi city. Int. J. Adv. Comput. Sci. Appl. **10**(3), 596–604 (2019)
23. Barthélemy, J., Carletti, T.: A dynamic behavioural traffic assignment model with strategic. Trans. Res. Part C **85**, 23–46 (2017)
24. Lowrie, P.R.: Scats. A traffic responsive method of controlling urban traffic, Sydney co-ordinated adaptive traffic system (1990)
25. Jian, Z., Tang, T.-Q., Yu, S.-W.: An improved car-following model accounting for the preceding car's taillight. Physica A: Stat. Mech. Appl. **492**, 1831–1837 (2018)

Design and Evaluations of Multi-agent Simulation Model for Electric Power Sharing Among Households

Yasutaka Nishimura[1]([✉]), Taichi Shimura[2], Kiyoshi Izumi[3], and Kiyohito Yoshihara[1]

[1] KDDI Research Inc., Saitama, Japan
yu-nishimura@kddi-research.jp
[2] Kozo Keikaku Engineering Inc., Tokyo, Japan
[3] The University of Tokyo, Tokyo, Japan

Abstract. Electric power sharing among households based on the bidding method is studied as a future service. In order to verify the feasibility of such a service, a new multi-agent simulation model has been designed. We validated this model through some evaluations. For example, it is confirmed that the market price on this service stably changes according to the supply-demand balance between both sold and purchased bid volumes. In addition to that, the results of the household profit and contract rate of this service showed that the design for bid strategies works as intended in most cases.

Keywords: Electric power sharing · Multi-agent simulation · Artificial market

1 Introduction

In Japan, the surplus power purchase system (FIT [Feed-in Tariff]) started in 2009 as part of the promotion of solar power generation (PV generation). FIT guarantees customers' surplus electricity obtained by subtracting residential consumption from PV generation purchased at a fixed unit price during 10 years. Therefore, households whose guarantee period ends (graduate FIT households) have appeared since November 2019. This guaranteed price has been lower year by year from 48 yen/kWh in 2009 to 26 yen/kWh in 2018. New surplus power purchase services for graduate FIT households have been announced by some electricity retailers, but the price is currently about 10 yen/kWh at most, and is expected to be significantly lower than the guaranteed price of FIT. For this reason, and in order to increase the value of surplus power in graduate FIT households, the promotion of self-consumption by introducing storage batteries and the sharing of electric power are being studied. The latter option allows households to sell surplus power to other households [1].

The electric power sharing principle is profitable to households if surplus electricity is sold to other households at a higher price than sold to the electricity retailer. Households that do not have PV can also benefit when they purchase electricity from other households at a lower price than the purchase price from the electricity retailer. One of the merits

S. Swarup and B. T. R. Savarimuthu (Eds.): MABS 2020, LNAI 12316, pp. 41–53, 2021.
https://doi.org/10.1007/978-3-030-66888-4_4

other than money is environmental value. For example, if households that do not have PV purchases electricity generated by PV from other households via the electric power sharing, their ratio of renewable energy can be increased.

As demand (total amount of surplus power from households) and supply (total amount of in-house consumption of households) do not always match, a method determining the trading partner for monetary value and environmental value of electricity is required. Such trading methods include the bidding method used for trading between power generation companies and electricity retailers on JEPX (Japan Electric Power Exchange) [2]. There is a possibility that the monetary value and the environmental value of electricity can be flexibly allocated according to the household's situation and values such as profit pursuit and eco-friendliness, through electric power sharing by the bidding method.

Since there is almost no existing service for electric power sharing, verification of service feasibility is required, such as the profits of households and electricity retailers, the stability of market prices, and the number of service subscribers required for market establishment. However, the bidding behavior of household changes depending on the environment such as weather and seasons, and interacts with the bidding of other households. This type of system is called as a complex system, and verification of the electric power sharing assuming bidding is not an easy task. One promising way to analyze such a complex system is to use MAS (Multi-Agent Simulation) [3].

In this paper, we present a MAS model for electrical power sharing designed for verifying the feasibility of electrical power sharing assuming bidding. One of the features of the proposed MAS model is that the bid strategy reflects the household's values such as profit pursuit and eco-friendliness. We validate our MAS model through some simulations under multiple conditions with varying PV ownership ratio, bid strategy ratio and so forth. Specifically, we confirm that market price stability. In addition, we confirm that household profits and contract rate are as expected, in order to see the potential of the electrical power sharing by bidding to allocate the monetary value and environmental value of electricity to households.

2 Related Works

As a main application example of MAS in the field of electric power and energy, there is research to evaluate and verify the new system concerning the electric power market and transmission and distribution system from the viewpoint of stability, efficiency and effectiveness. As for the electric power market, agent simulation is used in many researches in Japan and overseas [4, 5]. In the US, an agent-based large-scale electricity market test bed AMES has already been established and used for the evaluation and verification of the electricity market system [6].

Regarding power transmission and distribution systems, the efficiency of smart grid systems which determine the behavior of power consumption agents using actual home consumption data and PV power generation data is evaluated [7]. One study [8] verifies the effective use of PV generation and household profit, assuming power sharing via bidding among households in a small community. A bid strategy that changes the bid price depending on the available capacity of the storage battery has been modeled.

As described above, there are not many known examples of MAS application that assumes electricity sharing between households by bidding. The study [8] has similar assumptions, but the main purpose was the evaluation of effective use of PV generation and bid strategy covers battery status. On the other hand, the purpose of this paper is to verify the feasibility of the power sharing service. We have designed a MAS model that places emphasis on evaluation and verification from the service perspective, such as modeling different household's values, such as profit pursuit and eco-friendliness, and evaluating household profits. In addition, this paper examines the stability of market prices and changes in household profit when the ratio of bid strategies and the supply-demand balance are different.

3 Assumption of Electric Power Sharing

3.1 Outline of Electric Power Sharing Service

Electricity is purchased and sold through bidding from/to households. Buy and sell bids are each made of 48 frames a day, with 30 min as one frame, with reference to JEPX [2]. Each frame is given a frame ID (1 to 48). The electricity that can be sold is the surplus power of PV generation. Accordingly, PV-owned households can be sellers in the service. The electric power charged in the storage battery cannot be sold on the service. This is because reverse power flow of storage batteries is not currently allowed in Japan. All households can become buyers in the service. They can buy electricity from other households for in-house consumption.

3.2 Assumptions

Contract with Electricity Retaile
It is assumed that, in addition to the electric power sharing service, each household has contracted with an electricity retailer. In fact, it is not possible to cover the consumption of each household by electric power sharing alone, especially at night when there is no PV generation. In addition, considering that all selling bids may not be contracted, it is assumed that households that can be sellers have a contract with an electricity retailer for fixed price surplus purchase service.

Household's Values on Electricity
This paper considers three different values on electricity for a household: profit pursuit, eco-friendly, and indifference.

Profit pursuit households have an interest in money and seek to increase profits through electric power sharing. In fact, interest in money is expected to be high, since some retailers offer electricity services that highlight differences in electricity fee.

Eco-friendly households aim to improve their ratio of renewable energy consumption through electrical power sharing. It buys and sells via the electric power sharing with a price range that does not cause a loss compared to the fixed price of an electricity retailer. It is assumed that there are a certain number of eco-friendly households, since some retailers has launched electricity services with a high proportion of renewable energy. It is also expected that the number of eco-friendly households will increase in the future due to the growing interest in global warming and CO_2 reduction.

Indifference households do not care only if there is no loss compared to the fixed price of their electricity retailer. Households who joins the electricity power sharing service casually because they do not lose, or who have been less interested in the service over time.

Contract Method

A blind single price auction is considered as the contract method. This is because this auction is used in many electricity markets among electricity retailers and electricity power generation companies both at domestic and abroad, e.g., JEPX and EPEX (European Power Exchange). In addition, this auction has a feature that the market price at each frame time is determined as one. Hence, the market price can be considered as the electricity value of the frame. This makes it easy to analyze changes in market prices.

Electric Power Flow

There are two possible power flows. The first one is a direct electricity flow between households along with electric power sharing transactions. Second one is the virtual transaction of electric power sharing without changing the existing electric power flow. As the former requires large-scale renovation of the existing power infrastructure, it is unrealistic to assume that a wide range of electric power sharing will be performed. Therefore, this paper is considering the latter.

Transaction Flow

The household whose bid is contracted buys electricity from and sells to other households at a contract price. Households whose bid is not contracted buy and sell electricity at a fixed price from/to electricity retailers.

There are two ways to execute contract: (1) before and (2) after the time when electricity actually flows. In the first case, each household decides the amounts of bids based on the predicted values of in-house consumption and PV generation. The contract amount is determined based on this bid amount. If there is a prediction error in in-house consumption and PV generation, it may not be possible to buy and sell exactly as contracted, making transactions complicated. This paper is considering the second case, so that the amounts of bids are based on actual value, making transactions simple.

The flow from bidding to contract is shown in Fig. 1, taking as an example of a frame ID 20 (9:30 to 10:00) in one day. Selling households S1 and S2 and buying households B1 and B2 determine bid prices before 9:30 (Fig. 1(1)). The bid amount of each household is determined after the fact based on PV power generation and home consumption from 9:30 to 10:00 (Fig. 1(2)). The contract is then calculated based on the bid price and bid amount (Fig. 1(3)). Based on the price priority principle of the blind single price auction, a selling bid of 10 kWh from S1 and a buying bid of 10 kWh from B1 are contracted. The remaining S2's bid and B2's bid are not contracted because the bid prices do not match. Then, S2 sells its 10 kWh of electricity to an electricity retailer at a fixed price, and B2 buys the required 5 kWh of electricity from an electricity retailer at a fixed price.

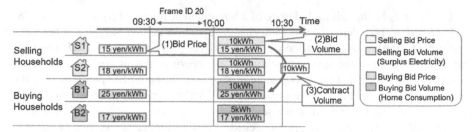

Fig. 1. Flow from bid to contract in the case of frame ID 20

4 Design of MAS Model

We designed a MAS model that simulates the electric power sharing and associated transactions. The model consists of household agents and an electricity retailer agent.

4.1 Household Agent

A household agent has three attributes information that can be set: the owned equipment, the contract information with the electricity retailer, and the bid strategy.

Owned Equipment
Information of owned equipment, such as PV and storage battery, can be set. If owned, specification information of the owned equipment such as the rated output value [kW] for PV and the capacity [kWh] for a storage battery is set.

Contract Information with Electricity Retailer
Information on the unit price of both electricity purchased from the electricity retailer [yen/kWh] and electricity sold to an electricity retailer [yen/kWh] is set. These unit prices can be set for each frame. This means that these can be a fixed value, regardless of the frame, or they can be different during the day and at night.

Bid Strategy
One strategy among profit pursuit, eco-friendliness, and indifference is selected as a bid strategy corresponding to the household's values on electricity. The household determines the bid price according to the selected bid strategy. Here, a buying bid price higher than the unit price of electricity purchased from an electricity retailer is irrational. Similarly, a selling bid price lower than the unit price of electricity sold to an electricity retailer is irrational. Therefore, common to all bidding strategies, the upper limit P_MAX of the bid price is the unit price of electricity purchased from the electricity retailer, and the lower limit P_MIN is the unit price of electricity sold to the electricity retailer.

Profit Pursuit
The profit pursuit strategy changes the bid price according to past contract results and market prices, in order to increase profit.

Let $bid(i, j)$ be the selling bid price of a household at frame ID $j(j = 1, 2, \cdots, 48)$ on day i. $bid(i, j)$ is calculated using information about the selling bid price of the same household for the previous day at the same frame $bid(i - 1, j)$, market price $MP(i - 1, j)$, and contract result of the same household for the previous day at the same frame, as shown in Fig. 2(a). If it is not contracted at the same frame on the previous day, the selling bid price is lowered by parameter a [yen/kWh] to facilitate the contract. On the other hand, if it is contracted at the same frame on the previous day, the difference between $MP(i - 1, j)$ and $bid(i, j)$ is checked. If this difference is less than or equal to the threshold α, the selling bid price is maintained. This is because it is relatively likely that the selling bid will not be contracted if the selling bid price is raised. Whereas, if the difference is larger than the threshold α, the selling bid price is probabilistically increased by a parameter b [yen/kWh] to increase profits. As a means of probabilistically increasing the selling bid price, a random number p (0 to 1) is used and it is increased when $p > threshold\ \beta$. Parameters a, b, α, and β are real number greater than 0, respectively.

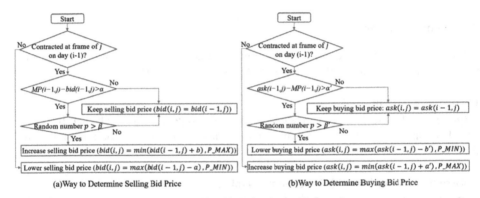

(a)Way to Determine Selling Bid Price   (b)Way to Determine Buying Bid Price

Fig. 2. Way to determine bid price for profit pursuit strategy

The buying bid price of the profit pursuit strategy $ask(i, j)$ is determined in a similar way to that for the selling bid price of a household $bid(i, j)$, using the buying bid price of the same household for the previous day at the same frame $ask(i - 1, j)$, market price $MP(i - 1, j)$, parameters a', b', α', and β', as shown in Fig. 2 (b). These parameters are real number greater than 0.

Eco-Friendly

The eco-friendly strategy always executes market orders to increase the contract rate. A market order is a bidding method that does not specify a bid price, and is contracted prior to a bid by other strategies that specify a bid price. Now, we consider the contract price for the bid of a market order. As with other bids that specify prices, if the contract price of the market order is also the market price, the market order is the optimal strategy for profit as well as for the contract rate. To make the bid strategy different for profit pursuit and eco-friendly, the contract price of the market order is set to the 80th percentile of the bid price of the bid contracted in the transaction. Hence, eco-friendly strategy is easier to be contracted, but its profit per contract is lower, compared to profit pursuit strategy.

Indifference
The indifference strategy always executes bidding at the same bid price.

Common to profit pursuit and indifference strategies, the initial bid price for each household is given as a uniform distribution between the unit price of electricity purchased from the electricity retailer and the unit price of electricity sold to the electricity retailer.

4.2 Electricity Retailer Agent

The electricity retailer agent aggregates both buying and selling bids of the household, and performs the contract calculation. Then, it notifies each household agent of its contract result and market price information. Based on the contract results, the electricity retailer aggregates both buying and selling volume as well as price through electric power sharing. In addition, the electricity retailer agent calculates buying and selling volumes via the electricity retailer. Finally, it calculates expenditures for electricity purchases and income from selling electricity for each household.

5   Basic Evaluation of Electric Power Sharing MAS Model

We have developed a MAS model for electrical power sharing based on the design described in Sect. 4. In this section, we validate the MAS model through some simulations.

5.1 Evaluation Policy

With the goal of using the model to verify the feasibility of the electric power sharing service, the validity of the model is confirmed through basic evaluation. Specifically, the following two points are confirmed.

1. The market price of electric power sharing is formed stably according to the supply and demand balance of the selling bid and the buying bid.
2. The household profit and contract rate for each profit pursuit, eco-friendly and indifferent bid strategy is as designed (Sect. 4.1 Bid Strategy).

5.2 Evaluation Indicator

The market price trend, supply and demand balance, household profit, and contract rate are used as evaluation indicators. The market price is calculated through the contract calculation by matching both buying bid and selling bid in each frame. The balance between supply and demand is calculated as (bid volume for selling [kWh]/bid volume for buying [kWh]). The balance between supply and demand is zero at night and increases with the increase in PV generation during the day.

For easy analysis, household profit is aggregated as the amount of money obtained by sharing electricity, starting from the income and expenditure when all electricity is bought and sold with an electricity retailer. As a result, the household profit is 0 yen or more. For example, the profit for households that do not buy or sell electricity through electric power sharing is 0 yen. The contract rate is calculated as the contract amount [kWh]/bid amount [kWh].

5.3 Input Data

Figure 3 shows an example of home consumption data, which is created by statistical processing based on actual home consumption data of an electrical service. On weekdays, there is a peak after getting up around frame ID from 15 to 17 (7:00–8:30), and it is decreased after going out around frame ID 18 (8:30–9:00). Whereas, on Saturdays, Sundays, and holidays, the peak due to wake-up is slower than on weekdays, and in-day home consumption tends to be higher than on weekdays.

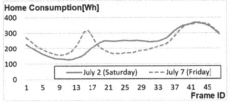

Fig. 3. Home consumption data   **Fig. 4.** PV generation data

Figure 4 shows an example of PV generation data. PV generation data was created from 1st July to 31st July in Tokyo, using numerical simulations using sunrise and sunset times and solar altitude information. The rated output of PV is set at 4 kW, which is a general level, and peaked at noon on the summer solstice, and other days and time zones are reduced according to the solar altitude. Reflecting the amount of sunshine on PV generation is a topic for future investigation.

5.4 Conditions for Basic Evaluation

Table 1 shows the conditions for the basic evaluation. The simulation period is 1 month from July 1 to July 31, and the number of households is 10,000. The unit price of electricity bought from an electricity retailer is 26 yen/kWh, and the unit price of electricity sold to an electricity retailer is 5 yen/kWh, with reference to the general price in Japan. These unit prices are fixed values common to 48 frames a day.

The ratios of bid strategy are 10:10:80 and 80:20:0 for profit pursuit strategy, eco-friendly strategy and indifference strategy. The former is for easy analysis, because indifference households which have the simplest bid strategy account for 80%. The latter is for one of realistic examples. Though some services providing green electricity with a little higher price have appeared even in japan, it is assumed that there are more profit pursuit household than eco-friendly household.

Table 1. Conditions for basic evaluation

Simulation period	1 month from July 1 to July 31
Number of households	10,000
Unit price of electricity bought from electricity retailer	26 yen/kWh
Unit price of electricity sold to electricity retailer	5 yen/kWh
PV ownership rate	2%, 10%, 20%
Bid strategy rate (Profit pursuit: Eco-friendly: Indifference)	10:10:80, 80:20:0

The PV ownership rate is set to 2%, 10% and 20%, in order to see changes in market prices and household profits when the supply-demand balance is different. Current ownership rate in Japan is around 2% and will be increased in the future for the purpose of CO_2 reduction. The ownership rate of storage batteries is assumed to be 0%, for the sake of facilitating analysis.

The parameters of the profit pursuit strategy have been set as follows, $a = 1$ yen/kWh, $b = 1$ yen/kWh, $\alpha = 3$ yen/kWh, and $\beta = 0.3$. $a' = 1$ yen/kWh, $b' = 1$ yen/kWh, $\alpha' = 3$ yen/kWh, and $\beta' = 0.3$.

5.5 Evaluation Results

Market Price Trends and Supply-Demand Balance
Figure 5 shows supply-demand balance for each frame in the first 10 days when the PV ownership rate is 2%, 10% and 20%. Figure 6 shows the market price trends in the first 10 days in case of bid strategy rate of 10:10:80. For the sake of simplicity, the market price of the frame where there is no contract is set at 0 yen/kWh. Regardless of the PV ownership ratio, the supply-demand balance is zero every night due to no PV generation. On the other hand, the supply-demand balance is larger than 0 and some bids are contracted from around 5:30 sunrise to around 18:00 sunset.

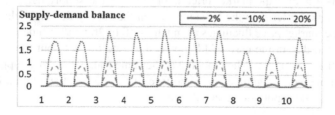

Fig. 5. Supply-demand balance of each frame

When the PV ownership rate is 2%, the supply-demand balance is in the range of 0 to 0.19, and the selling bid volume is extremely small, at most 1/5 of the buying bid volume. The market price is relatively high and ranges from 22.0 to 26.0 yen/kWh. In

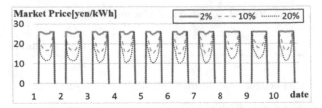

Fig. 6. Market price of each frame (bid strategy rate of 10:10:80)

the case of the PV ownership rate being 10%, the supply-demand balance is in the range of 0 to 1.11, and there are frames where the selling bid amount exceeds the buying bid amount. The market price is in the wide range of 14.9–26.0 yen/kWh. When the PV ownership rate is 20%, the supply-demand balance is in the range of 0 to 2.48, and there is a frame where the selling bid amount is 2.48 times the buying bid amount. The market price is 10.0–26.0 yen/kWh, which is more widespread than when PV is 10%.

Next, Fig. 7 shows the daily market price trends of some frames when the PV ownership rate is 20%. The sunrise (Frame ID 11) and sunset (Frame ID 36) have a higher market price than 20 yen/kWh. This is because the supply-demand balance is small due to the low amount of PV generation. During that time (Frame ID 18, 24, 30), both the PV generation amount and the supply-demand balance are large, hence the market price is around 10-15 yen/kWh.

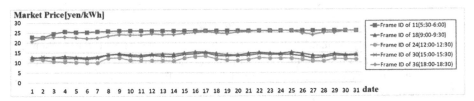

Fig. 7. Daily market price trends of some frames (bid strategy rate of 10:10:80, PV ownership rate is 20%)

As described above, the market price is high when the supply-demand balance is low, and the market price is in the low range when the supply-demand balance is high. In addition, the market price fluctuates as much as 10 to 26 yen/kWh depending on the Frame ID in one day in the case of PV ownership rate of 20%, but the daily market price of each frame is stable. When looking at the same frame, the daily supply-demand balance does not change significantly. Therefore, it can be said that the market price is stably formed by the supply-demand balance.

Household Profit

Figure 8 shows household average profit [yen/month] for each bid strategy for households with and without PV. In case of the bid strategy ratio of 10:10:80, regardless of the PV ownership rate, the profit of pursuit profit is the largest, as designed. In case of the bid strategy ratio of 80:20:0, there are two cases in which eco-friendly is more profitable than profit pursuit. We will analyze these cases in Sect. 5.6.

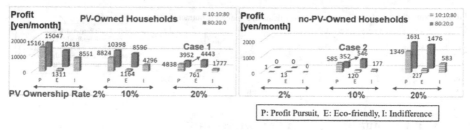

Fig. 8. Profit of PV-owned and non-PV-owned households for each bid strategy

As the PV ownership rate increases, the profits of PV-owned households become smaller, while the profits of non-PV-owned households become larger. This is consistent with the result (Fig. 5) that the market price shifts to a lower range as the PV ownership rate increases.

Contract Rate

Figure 9 shows the contract rate for each bid strategy for PV-owned and non-PV-owned households. Regardless of the bid strategy rate and the PV ownership rate, the eco-friendly contract rate is the largest, and the results are as designed. As the PV ownership rate is higher, the contracted rate of PV-owned households is lower, while the contracted rate of non-PV-owned households increase. This is consistent with the fact that the higher the PV ownership rate, the greater the supply-demand balance (Fig. 5).

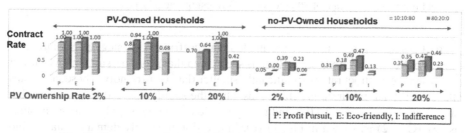

Fig. 9. Contract rate for each bid strategy (bid strategy rate of 10:10:80)

5.6 Analysis

Profit pursuit gets the largest profit under many conditions, but eco-friendly profits may be higher under certain conditions (Fig. 8 Case 1 and Case 2). We analyze these cases. Figure 10 and 11 show the profit and the contract rate for each frame in Case 1 and Case 2, respectively. Figure 10 (a) indicates that the magnitude relationship between the profit pursuit and eco-friendly is switched by the frame in Case 1. Figure 11 (a) shows that the eco-friendly profit is larger than the profit pursuit in all the frames in Case 2. Figure 10 (a) and Fig. 11 (a) also show that there was a big gap in the contract rate between eco-friendly and profit pursuit.

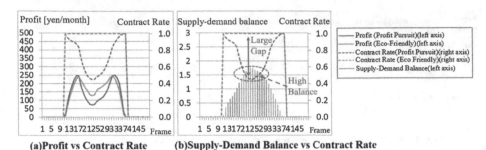

(a)Profit vs Contract Rate   (b)Supply-Demand Balance vs Contract Rate

Fig. 10. Profit and contract rate for each bid strategy for each frame in Case 1 (PV-owned household for bid strategy rate of 80:20:0 for PV ownership rate of 20%)

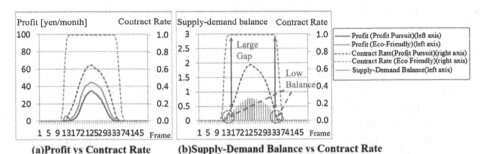

(a)Profit vs Contract Rate   (b)Supply-Demand Balance vs Contract Rate

Fig. 11. Profit and contract rate for each bid strategy for each frame in Case 2 (non-PV-owned household for bid strategy rate of 80:20:0 for PV ownership rate of 10%)

Profit pursuit strategy is more profitable than eco-friendly strategy per contract, as designed in Sect. 4.1 Bid Strategy. But it is speculated that profit pursuit obtains a lower profit when the contract rate is significantly smaller than eco-friendly. These large gaps in the contract rate occurred in selling bids when the supply-demand balance was high (Case 1) as shown in Fig. 10 (b), and in buying bids when the supply-demand balance was low (Case 2) as shown in Fig. 11 (b). In addition to supply-demand balance, bid strategy ratios will be compared. In the case of a bid strategy ratio of 10:10:80, profit pursuit households were able to maintain the contract rate and profits by contracting with indifferent households, which accounted for the majority. In the case of a bid strategy ratio of 80:20:0, the profit pursuing households that occupy the majority contend for profits, and the contract rate is considered to have declined. As a result, the profit of eco-friendly household becomes larger than that of profit pursuit household.

We can conclude from the above the bid strategy for eco-friendly households always follows the market order. On the other hand, it turned out that the bid strategy for profit pursuit may change depending on the supply-demand balance and the ratio of bid strategies of other participants.

6 Conclusion

In order to verify the feasibility of electric power sharing service, we newly designed a multi-agent simulation model. One of the features of the proposed MAS model is that the bid strategy reflects the household's values such as profit pursuit and eco-friendliness. Through evaluations of the MAS model, it is confirmed that the market price on this service stably changes according to the supply-demand balance. In addition to that, the results of household profit and contract rate of this service showed that the design for bid strategies works in most conditions. This mean that the monetary value and the environmental value of electricity can be allocated according to the household's values such as profit pursuit and eco-friendliness. The optimal bid strategy for profit pursuit may change depending on the supply-demand balance and the ratio of bid strategies, and the new bid strategy that can increase profits under various conditions is a subject for future study. Evaluations with various ratios of both bid strategy and PV ownership are also future works.

References

1. Sousa, T., Soares, T., Pinson, P., Moret, F., Baroche, T., Sorin, E.: Peer-to-peer and community-based markets: A comprehensive review. Renew. Sustain. Energy Rev. **104**, 367–378 (2019)
2. JEPX (Japan Electric Power Exchange). http://www.jepx.org/english/index.html
3. Matsui, T., Izumi, K., Drogoul, A., Gaudou, B., Marilleau, N.: Agent-based simulation for complex systems: Application to economics, finance, and social sciences. Pract. Multi-agent Syst. Stud. Comput. Intell. **325**(2011), 145–147 (2010)
4. Setsuya, K., Wander J.: An electricity market game using agent-based gaming technique for understanding energy transition. In: Proc. of 9th International Conference on Agents and Artificial Intelligence (ICAART 2017), Porto, Portugal, vol. 1, pp. 314–321, 2017-02-24/26 (2017)
5. Qudrat-Ullah, H.: Energy Policy Modeling in the 21st Century. Springer, New York (2013)
6. Sun, J., Tesfatsion, L.: Dynamic testing of whole-sale power market designs: An opensource agent-based framework. Comput. Econ. **30**(3), 291–327 (2007)
7. Vytelingum, P., Voice, T. D., Ramchurn, S., Rogers, A., Jennings, N.: Agent-based micro-storage management for the smart grid. In: Proceedings Autonomous Agents and Multiagent Systems, pp. 39–46 (2010)
8. Borislava, S., Kawamoto, D., Takefuji, Y.: Evaluation of the effects of bidding strategy with customized pricing on the individual Prosumer in a local energy market. Adv. Sci. Technol. Eng. Syst. J. **4**(4), 366–379 (2019)

Active Screening on Recurrent Diseases Contact Networks with Uncertainty: A Reinforcement Learning Approach

Han Ching Ou[⊠], Kai Wang, Finale Doshi-Velez, and Milind Tambe

Harvard University, Cambridge, MA 02138, USA
{hou,kaiwang,final,milind_tambe}@g.harvard.edu

Abstract. Controlling recurrent infectious diseases is a vital yet complicated problem. A large portion of the controlling epidemic relies on patients visit clinics voluntarily. However, they may already transmit the disease to their contacts by the time they feel sick enough to visit the clinic, especially for conditions with a long incubation period. Therefore, active screening/case finding was deployed to provide a powerful yet expensive means to control disease spread in recent years. To make active screening success a given limit budget, one of the challenges that need to be addressed is that we do not know the exact state of each patient. Given the number of horizon and budget we have in each time step, we also need to plan our screening efficiently and screening the vital patients in time. Thus, we apply a reinforcement learning approach to solve active screening problems on the network SIS disease model. The first contribution of this work is that we identify three significant challenges in active screening problems: partially observable states, combinatorial action choice, high-dimensional state-action space. We further propose the corresponding solutions to overcome these challenges. Specifically, we resolve the issue of high-dimensional state-action space by encoding the actions and partially observable states into a lower dimension form, which is done by either manually, using domain expertise, or automatically, using the state of the art GCN approach. We show that our approach can scale up to large graphs and perform decently compared to other baselines of previous literature and current practice.

1 Introduction

Contagious diseases, such as influenza and sexually transmitted diseases (STDs) (e.g., gonorrhea and chlamydia) are critical public-health challenges that continue to threaten lives and impose significant economic burden on society. For example, the economic loss due to influenza in the USA alone is estimated to be \$11.2 billion in 2015 [14]. While low-cost treatment programs are available, individuals ignore symptoms and delay care, increasing transmission risk. As a result, health agencies engage in active screening or contact tracing efforts, where individuals are asked to undergo diagnostic tests and offered treatment if tests are positive [5,7]. However, active screening is expensive in developing countries. Even in USA, Braxton et al. [4] state that "In 2012, 52% of state and local STD programs experienced budget cuts. This amounts to reductions in

© Springer Nature Switzerland AG 2021
S. Swarup and B. T. R. Savarimuthu (Eds.): MABS 2020, LNAI 12316, pp. 54–65, 2021.
https://doi.org/10.1007/978-3-030-66888-4_5

clinic hours, contact tracing, and screening for common STDs." Efficiently identifying and intervening for infectious cases is therefore of vital importance.

However, in many settings, active screening/contact tracing is expensive and time consuming. There is a huge body of literature on spread and control of recurrent diseases (no permanent immunity). However, all these prior work assume perfect observation of who is infected and who is not. Also, most of these methods focus on eradication of disease, which is not possible if the screening resources are limited. Thus, important real world characteristics such as partial observation and limited resources have not been handled in any prior work.

2 Problem Statement

In this work, we aim to use reinforcement learning to decide which patients to actively screen in each time frame for a multi-round scenario with limited horizon. The environment we considered is based on the well-known SIS model [1,2]. An individual can either be in state S (a healthy individual *susceptible* to disease) or I (the individual is *infected*). SIS models capture the dynamics of recurrent diseases, where permanent immunity is not possible (e.g., TB, typhoid). We adopt a discrete time SIS model for modeling the disease dynamics propagating on a given graph $G = (V, E)$, where each node represents a single patient and each edge indicates the link between people which disease can spread. We assume the structure of the contact network G to be known yet the states of patients to be unknown. We can only observe the patients' current states while actively screening the patients. At each round, we have k resources that allow us to provide active screening to k patients. After being screened, the infected patients recover back to susceptible healthy patients, while the susceptible patients remain susceptible.

Given a contact network $G(V, E)$, infection spreads via the edges in the network. There are $|V|$ individuals, and we use $\delta(v)$ to denote neighbors of node v in the network. Each individual (node) v in the network at time t is in state $\mathbf{s}_v(t) \in \{S, I\}$. Let $\mathbf{t}_v(t)$ denote the state vector that represents the true state of node v at time t where S is represented as $[1, 0]^\top$ and I as $[0, 1]^\top$. Given the initial state, an infected node infects its healthy neighbors with rate α independently and recovers with probability c. The latter term represents the probability that the node may visit a doctor on its own initiative. The health state transition probabilities of a node is then given by $P\left[s_v(t + 1) = \{S, I\}\right] = \mathbf{T}_v^N(t)\mathbf{t}_v(t)$ where

Table 1. Notations

Notations	Definition
Model	
S	susceptible state
I	infected state
α	transmission rate
c	cure rate
t	time step number
T	terminal time step
k	budget for each time step
$\delta(v)$	set of v's neighbors
$\mathbf{s}_v(t)$	state of v at time t
$\mathbf{a}(t)$	set of nodes actively screened as action
$\mathbf{o}(t)$	set of nodes naturally cured as observation
$\mathbf{t_v}(t)$	true state vector of node v at time t
$\mathbf{T}_v^N(t)$	true state transition matrix for $V \setminus a(t)$
$\mathbf{T}_v^A(t)$	true state transition matrix for $a(t)$
Algorithm	
$b_v(t)$	marginal probability of v being in I state
$b(t)$	belief vector of all nodes being in I state
$\mathbf{b}(t)$	intermediate belief vector after knowing $o(t)$
$\mathbf{B}_v^N(t)$	transition matrix for $V \setminus a(t) \cup o(t)$
$\mathbf{B}_v^A(t)$	transition matrix for $a(t) \cup o(t)$

$$\mathbf{T}_v^N(t) = \begin{array}{c} \\ S \\ I \end{array}\begin{array}{c} S \qquad\quad I \\ \left[\begin{matrix} 1 - q_v & c \\ q_v & 1 - c \end{matrix}\right] \end{array}, \qquad (1)$$

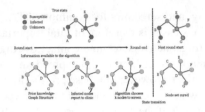

Fig. 1. The procedure of the ACTS problem.

and $q_v = 1 - (1 - \alpha)^{|\{u \in \delta(v) \mid s_u(t)=I\}|}$. The columns denote the state of v at time t and the rows denote the state at $t + 1$. The transition probabilities follow the disease dynamics described earlier. In particular, q_v captures the exact probability that node v becomes infected from its infected neighbors $\{u \in \delta(v) \mid s_u(t) = I\}$ and c captures the probability that I individuals recover without active screening.

Given such transition probabilities and an initial state, if no intervention happens, the network state evolves by flipping biased coins for each node to determine their next true state in each round. The process is repeated until the terminal step T is reached.

Motivated by active screening/contact tracing campaigns that have been practiced since the 1980s [5] and applied in various forms/diseases [4], we propose the Active Screening (ACTS) Problem. Given the SIS model in the previous section, an active screening agent seeks to determine the best node sets $a(t) \subset V$ to actively screen and cure with a limited budget of $|a(t)| \leq k$ at each round t. The agent does not know the ground truth health state of all individuals. The agent knows the network structure $G(V, E)$, the infection probability α, and recovery probability c. In addition, the agent observes the *naturally cured* node set $o(t)$ at time t—because this set of patients come to the clinic voluntarily. Active screening starts after the agent acquires information about $o(t)$. Let $a(t)$ be the set of nodes that are actively screened at time t. A node $v \in a(t)$ becomes cured at time $t + 1$. Thus, the transition matrix for a node $v \in a(t)$ is $P[s_v(t + 1) = \{S, I\}] = T_v^A(t)t_v(t)$, where

$$
T_v^A(t) = \begin{array}{c} \\ S \\ I \end{array} \begin{array}{c} S \quad I \\ \begin{bmatrix} 1 & 1 \\ 0 & 0 \end{bmatrix} \end{array} \tag{2}
$$

The action the agent takes at time t does not affect the transition matrix $T_v^N(t)$ of the nodes not involved in active screening.

Figure 1 illustrates an example of the problem procedure. The upper part of the figure shows how the true state of the network evolves and the lower part of the figure shows the information available to the algorithm. In this example, there are seven nodes A~G. In each round, infected nodes (nodes B, D, and G in the example) flip a coin and report to the clinic with probability c. The algorithm acquires the information of the nodes that eventually report to the clinic and are about to be cured, which is {G} this round. Based on this information, the algorithm will choose a set of nodes, say {D}, to actively screen. These two sets of nodes are guaranteed to be in S state in the next round. After that, the state of the network transitions and the next round starts.

It is worth noting that although both the nodes that voluntarily report to the clinic and the nodes that are actively screened are guaranteed to be in S state in the next round, their neighbors may still be infected by them in the current round. In the example, node E is infected by node D even though node D was actively screened. This allows us to simplify the state transitions because curing and spreading infection occur at the same time.

Our objective is to maximize the health quality of each individual at each round (in contrast to past work, which primarily focuses on the cost of eradicating the disease entirely). The objective of the ACTS problem is:

$$\min_{C_a(0),...,C_a(T)} \mathbb{E}\left[\sum_{t=0}^{T} \gamma^t \sum_{v \in V} \mathbb{1}_{\mathbf{s}_v(t)=I}\right]. \tag{3}$$

where $0 \leq \gamma \leq 1$ is a future discount factor.

Problem Statement *(ACTS Problem) Given a contact network $G(V, E)$, the disease and active screening model, find an active screening policy such that the expectation of $\sum_{t=0}^{T} \sum_{v \in V} \mathbb{1}_{\mathbf{s}_v(t)=I}$ is minimized.*

3 Challenges

In this paper, we first identify three main challenges that we are facing in ACTS problem.

- (a) Partially observable states
- (b) Combinatorial maximization problem
- (c) High-dimensional state-action space

The first challenge corresponds to the standard challenge in partially observable Markov decision process (POMDP), where the state is unknown and only a partial state can be observed by the agent. There are some POMDP solvers but the common issue of these solvers is the scalability. POMDP solvers are extremely unscalable, which are not suitable for our case as we have a large state and action space. The second issue comes along with large and combinatorial action choices. Any subset of patients with less than k elements is a feasible action, which can involve exponentially many actions and is hard to find the optimal action. The action selection problem can also be treated as a combinatorial problem, where our goal is to select the optimal k patients to provide active screening. In general, combinatorial maximization in active screening problem can be NP-hard to solve. Therefore, an efficient greedy algorithm is needed in our case, which will be discussed in the following section. The final challenge is the large state-action space. This corresponds to the issue of representation, where we require a compact representation of our state-action pair, while at the same time maintaining the information included in these state-action pairs. We will address these challenges in the following sections with our proposed solutions.

4   Partially Observable States

The first issue is that we do not have access to the hidden state, falling into the category of partially observable Markov decision process (POMDP), which prohibits the standard reinforcement learning methods to work here. There are also POMDP solvers that can directly solve a POMDP with partially observable states. However, these POMDP solvers are generally extremely slow and non-scalable. In our setting, the scale of our problem is quite large. We have $|V|$ hidden states, where each patient corresponds to an entry of the hidden state. POMDP solvers do not apply to such high dimensional setting, which urges us to think of other method to resolve the issue of partially observable state.

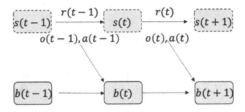

Fig. 2. Belief update based on action, observation, and previous state.

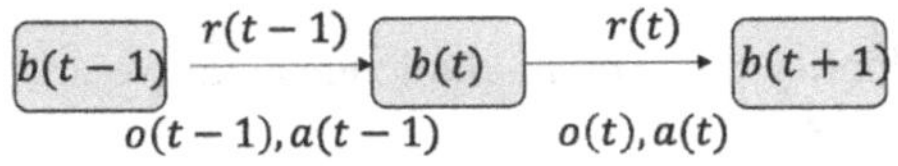

$$b(t-1) \xrightarrow[o(t-1),a(t-1)]{r(t-1)} b(t) \xrightarrow[o(t),a(t)]{r(t)} b(t+1)$$

Fig. 3. MDP on the belief state.

Solution: The way we resolve this issue is to use the posterior belief $\mathbf{b}(t)$ estimate of the current state $\mathbf{s}(t)$ as our fake state, which might lose some information but hopefully is rich enough to represent the original state distribution. The posterior belief $\mathbf{b}(t)$ at time t is affected by the previous observation $\mathbf{o}(t-1)$, action $\mathbf{a}(t-1)$, and belief $\mathbf{b}(t-1)$. As shown in Fig. 2, we can denote the belief update function as $\mathbf{b}(t) = g(\mathbf{b}(t-1), \mathbf{a}(t-1), \mathbf{o}(t-1))$. Now this update function is achieved by an approximate Bayesian approach, where people have been actively screened or observed in the clinic in the last round will be healthy in this round, and the people with no information can be updated by the conditional probability.

Once we get the posterior belief, we can use the belief as our new state, then run basic online reinforcement learning methods afterward. The new MDP structure is shown in Fig. 3.

5   Combinatorial Maximization Problem

The second issue is that we cannot easily compute the optimal action $\max_{\mathbf{a} \in A} Q(\mathbf{b}, \mathbf{o}, \mathbf{a})$. Notice that since this is in the partially observable setting, so at the beginning of each round, an observation $\mathbf{o}$ will be given and can be used to determine the

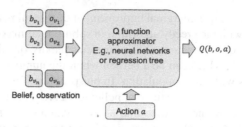

Fig. 4. Q function with belief, observation, and action as inputs. The function predicts a single scalar value as the Q value of the given belief, observation, and action.

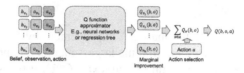

Fig. 5. Q function with belief and observation as inputs and with marginal improvement of selecting each patient as output. The predicted reward of a given action can be computed by taking summation of the marginal improvement of curing patients in the action.

action. Given the exponential size of all feasible actions A, the maximization problem is a combinatorial optimization problem, which can be computationally expensive to solve. The way we try to resolve the issue is to employ different greedy algorithms. An incorrect estimate of the maximum value Q value could lead to incorrect equilibrium of Bellman equation, which might break the optimality of the equilibrium of Bellman equation.

Solution: Our proposed solution here is to predict the improvement of each individual patient selection instead of an aggregated improvement of the entire set of patients. As shown in Fig. 4, the standard Q function takes belief and observation (state), and action as inputs, and outputs a single scalar value as the predicted future reward after taking this action. Instead, as shown in Fig. 5, our Q function outputs a scalar for each individual patient, representing the predicted marginal improvement if we actively screen this patient. By doing so, the optimization problem becomes much easier, where we can directly estimate the improvement of screening an additional patient, which only requires one additional access to the Q function. Nonetheless, this approach ignores the correlation between patients. It also assumes the reward of an entire action is separable into marginal improvement from each patients been screened. However, given the hardness of the original combinatorial maximization problem, we have to sacrifice some accuracy in exchange of the scalability. Using the Q function with marginal improvement outputs, we will show two heuristics in the following section.

5.1 Incremental Selection

The first heuristic method is to incrementally add patients into the screening set until we run out of the budget. Given the existing action, we can feed the action into the Q function to re-estimate the new marginal improvement of screening all the other patients again. This is aligned with the greedy algorithm in submodular maximization problems, which has a nice theoretical guarantee. The time complexity of this heuristic is linear in terms of the budget k, which can be a burden when the number of budget increases, especially in networks with large population. In our problem, for each iteration of new episode or each gradient update on a tuple of belief, observation, action, and next belief, we require to run the above heuristic to find an approximate optimal next action with time complexity $O(k)$. Although each iteration is not too expensive, in the reinforcement learning domain, iteratively training on this heuristic is still quite expensive.

5.2 One-Shot Selection

Instead of iteratively updating the marginal improvement by the updated action, we can directly select the top k patients with the largest marginal improvement. This only requires one single evaluation with time complexity $O(1)$. It is also less accurate due to the one-shot selection. However, we can see a significant speedup while using this simplified heuristic.

A mixture of these two heuristics is to iteratively select a batch of patients and update the resulting predictions afterward. It can balance between the accuracy and the scalability, which is left as a future direction.

6   High-Dimensional State-Action Space

In Fig. 5, in order to estimate the $Q(\mathbf{b}, \mathbf{o}, \mathbf{a})$ value, we need to feed the belief $\mathbf{b}$, observation $\mathbf{o}$, and action $\mathbf{a}$ into the Q function, which is a high-dimensional vector. From the function approximation perspective, in order to learn from high-dimensional data, the sample complexity could be much larger than of low-dimensional data. In the reinforcement learning domain, it corresponds to the need of a huge amount of data to collect and learn from. This is generally infeasible in the offline case and time consuming in the online case. Therefore, we would like to have a compact representation but at the same time maintaining the information containing in the input.

We first show a failed attempt and then show another two alternatives that we eventually use.

6.1   One-Hot Encoding

One naive and straightforward encoding method is to use one-hot encoding to encode action and observation. This means we will have three vectors of length $|V|$, which are $\mathbf{b}, \mathbf{o}$ where $\mathbf{o}_v = 1$ if node v is observed and 0 and $\mathbf{a}$ where $\mathbf{a}_v = 1$ if node v is selected and 0 otherwise. Then we simply concatenate into one single vector with length $3|V|$ and feed into our regression model.

However, this encoding method has many drawbacks. First, the dimension is high. Second, it is hard for the regress to learn the close relationship of the i-th, $i + |V|$-th and $i + 2|V|$-th elements in the state vector, as they represents the same node. Finally, the encoding method did not encode the fact that the observation and action set of nodes (o and a) are guaranteed to be cured in the next round and again relies the reinforcement learning to figure that out. Given there are a great amount of information to learn, this encoding method is not applicable due to its requirement of intensive amount of training to reason the relations between its high dimensional features.

Therefore, we propose the following two alternatives.

6.2 Nodewise Encoding

Since feeding all the features at once is not working, an intuitive way is to consider each node independently as shown in Fig. 6, where we feed the features related to node v to the Q function to get the predicted marginal improvement of actively screening node v. In order to take the graph structure into account, we can also include some local graph features as the features related to node v, e.g., the degree of node v, average path length starting from v etc. The belief, observation, action, and the graph features of node v are fed into the Q function and get a single scalar value, representing the prediction of node v. This can largely reduce the size of input by including only the features related to the corresponding nodes. However, we know that the disease can spread from nodes to their neighbors, which implies that we cannot simply ignore the neighbor nodes and their features. Although such abrupt reduction can efficiently reduce the dimension, it can lose a significant amount of information and graph structure at the same time.

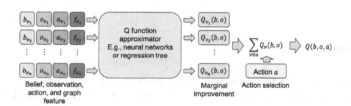

Fig. 6. Instead of feeding all the features into a single Q function estimator, we can feed each node-dependent feature only into the Q function estimator to reduce the dimensionality.

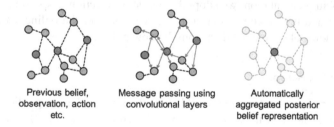

Fig. 7. Message passing in the convolutional layers can allow features like belief, observation, and action to propagate to the neighbor nodes.

6.3 Graph Convolutional Neural Networks

Another more structural ways to encode the features is to apply graph convolutional neural networks (GCNs) [11]. We can encode the features related to node v as the node features of v. The convolutional layers in GCNs can facilitate the nature of message passing and automatically aggregate the neighbor features as shown in Fig. 7. By using GCNs, we do not need to hand-craft graph features to represent the graph structure. What we need to do is to make GCNs learn the underlying graph embedding and form the corresponding representation.

Figure 8 demonstrates the flowchart of our GCN implementation. We replace the Q function estimator by a GCN, which takes node features and the graph as input and outputs a prediction for each node in the graph.

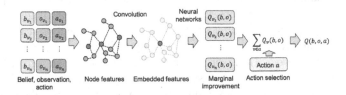

Fig. 8. Integrating GCN as our Q function can resolve the issue of high-dimensional input and also automatically extract the graph structure and form a compact feature embedding.

7 Experiments

In this project, we implement the two different encodings mentioned in Sect. 6. For the nodewise encoding, we follow the implementation of fitted Q learning [8] with extra trees regressor [9] as the Q function approximator. For the GCN encoding, we implement a deep Q network (DQN) [12] with GCN proposed by Morris et al. [13], where we maintain a fixed-size replay memory to continuously train the GCN. For both FQI and DQN implementation, we adopt the one-shot selection to speed up finding the optimal action and the maximization problem. We consider the online setting, where we can apply new policy and get data from the new policy.

7.1 Experiment Setup

We perform our experiments on real world contact networks that are publicly available. We set our finite horizon to be $T = 20$ which represents about 10 years of active screening with each period being six months [6]. We set the discount factor of 0.9. We assume $(\alpha, c) = (0.1, 0.1)$ and the network structure is known by surveys or estimations and set our budget k to be 10% of the population n in each period, thus the algorithm needs to scale well according to budget as graph size grows. Finally, we set the random policy probability to be $\epsilon = 0.05$ in our learning process.

We compare the following screening strategies with our reinforcement learning algorithm

(1a) RANDOM: Randomly select nodes for active screening.
(1b) MAXDEGREE: Successively choose nodes with the largest degree until the budget is reached.
(1c) EIGENVALUE: Greedily choose nodes that reduce the largest eigenvalue of **A** the most until the budget is reached.

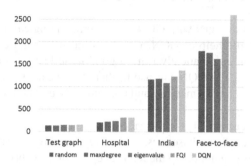

Fig. 9. Reward of different methods on different dataset over 10 times average.

Other then simulated graph, we evaluate the performance on the following realistic contact networks which is collected from diverse sources. The networks are carefully selected to have significant variation in size $|V|$, average degree d, average shortest path length ρ_L, assortativity ρ_D and epidemic threshold (spectral radius) $\frac{1}{\lambda_A^*}$ as table 2 shows.

(2a) **Test graph** we use the spatial preferential attachment model to generate a graph of 20 nodes. Such approach has the heavy-tailed degree distributions observed in many real networks.
(2b) **Hospital** [15]: A dense contact network collected in a university hospital to study the path of disease spread.
(2c) **India** [3]: A human contact network collected from a rural village in India where active screening with limited budget may take place.
(2d) **Face-to-face** [10]: A network describing face-to-face behavior during the exhibition INFECTIOUS: STAY AWAY in 2009 at the Science Gallery in Dublin, in which influenza might spread through close contact of individuals.

7.2 Experiment Result

In Fig. 9, we can see that our implementation of FQI with simple nodewise feature embedding can outperform all the other baselines. Notice that the *maxdegree* baseline can also be treated as another simple nodewise

Table 2. Properties of the contact network data sets.

Network	$|V|$	$\frac{1}{\lambda_A^*}$	d	ρ_L	ρ_D
Hospital [15]	75	0.027	15.19	1.60	-0.18
India [3]	202	0.095	3.43	3.11	0.02
Face-to-face [10]	410	0.042	6.74	3.63	0.23

feature embedding if we use the node
degree as the only feature and with a
simple Q function which directly returns the node degree as the predicted marginal
improvement. This *maxdegree* baseline performs quite poorly as it ignores the belief,
observation, and action, leading to a myopic action selection with poor performance.
In our FQI implementation, we train a regression tree to select and extract important
features to make the prediction, which allows us to deal with various features in a more
elegant way.

Our second algorithm DQN with GCN feature embedding can further improve the
solution quality. With the help of GCN, we do not need to hand-craft graph features
of each node. GCN can automatically learn a good node features embedding and use
them to make prediction. The DQN can also further improve the scalability and solution
quality by maintaining a replay memory and continuously update the memory and train
on it.

As presented, we can see that after encoding belief, observation, and the action,
our approaches exceed all the baselines. By either manually extracting node related
features or automatically maintaining the feature representation through GCN, FQI with
regression tree and nodewise encoding (manually) and DQN with GCN (automatically)
outperform other baselines.

Overall, as the graph size increases, we can also observe more improvement against
the standard baselines. However, we are still facing the issues of scalability, where our
implementations of FQI and DQN require a long training time compared to all other
myopic baselines. The memory requirement of DQN is also another issue. We will
leave the scalability issue as our future direction. Hopefully these reinforcement learning based approaches can be applied to larger networks and have a real impact to our
society.

8   Conclusion

We implement reinforcement learning on an active screening model by encoding the
high dimension action and state with large solution space into a low dimension, infor-
mative representation. This can be done either manually (FQI) or automatically (DQN).
"Teaching" the regressor by efficiently encode information using domain knowledge
helps improve the performance and reduce the amount of training needed. The future
direction of this work is to scale our solution to even larger networks with millions of
nodes and reach higher performance by overcoming the trade-off we made for scalability.

9   Appendix

9.1   Belief Update

First, we can encode $a(t)$ into $b(t)$ using our knowledge toward the model. From the
model, we know that the node set in $o(t)$ are resulted from infected nodes report with
probability c. Using the Bayesian posterior probability, we can update the original belief
vector to a intermediate belief vector $\bar{b}(t)$ as have

$$\bar{b}_v(t) = \begin{cases} 1, & v \in o(t) \\ \frac{(1-c)b_v(t)}{(1-\mathbf{b}_v(t))+(1-c)\mathbf{b}_v(t)}, & otherwise \end{cases} \tag{4}$$

Next, we need to encode the action $a(t)$ and the fact that set $o(t) \cup a(t)$ are guaranteed to be cured in the next round. To accomplish this, we simply update the intermediate belief state $\bar{b}(t)$ to the prediction of belief in the next round $\mathbf{b}(t+1)$ and use it as our state representation.

$$b_v(t+1) = \begin{cases} 0, & v \in o(t) \cup a(t), \\ p_v(1-x_v)+x_v, & otherwise \end{cases} \tag{5}$$

where $p_v = 1 - \prod_{u \in \delta(v)}(1 - \alpha \bar{b}_u(t))$ and $\delta(v)$ represent the neighbor of v. This maintance and update our belief of the next time step $\mathbf{b}(t+1)$.

References

1. Anderson, R.M., May, R.M.: Infectious Diseases of Humans: Dynamics and Control. Oxford University Press, Oxford (1992)
2. Bailey, N.T.: The Mathematical Theory of Infectious Diseases and its Applications. Charles Griffin & Company Ltd., Glasgow (1975)
3. Banerjee, A., Chandrasekhar, A.G., Duflo, E., Jackson, M.O.: The diffusion of microfinance. Science, **341** (2013)
4. Braxton, J., et al.: Sexually transmitted disease surveillance 2016. In: CDC (2017)
5. Cadman, D., Chambers, L., Feldman, W., Sackett, D.: Assessing the effectiveness of community screening programs. JAMA, **251** (1984)
6. CDC: Tuberculosis: General information. MMWR. Recommendations and reports: Morbidity and mortality weekly report (2011). https://www.cdc.gov/tb/publications/factsheets/general/tb.pdf
7. Eames, K.T., Keeling, M.J.: Contact tracing and disease control. Proc.R. Soc. Lond. Ser. B, Biol. Sci. **270**, 2563 (2003)
8. Ernst, D., Geurts, P., Wehenkel, L.: Tree-based batch mode reinforcement learning. J. Mach. Learn. Res. **6**, 503–556, April 2005
9. Geurts, P., Ernst, D., Wehenkel, L.: Extremely randomized trees. Mach. Learn. **63**(1), 3–42 (2006)
10. Isella, L., Stehlé, J., Barrat, A., Cattuto, C., Pinton, J.F., Van den Broeck, W.: What's in a crowd? analysis of face-to-face behavioral networks. J. Theor. Biol. **271** (2011)
11. Kipf, T.N., Welling, M.: Semi-supervised classification with graph convolutional networks. In: ICLR-17. Toulon (2017)
12. Mnih, V., et al.: Playing atari with deep reinforcement learning. arXiv preprint arXiv:1312.5602 (2013)
13. Morris, C., et al.: Weisfeiler and leman go neural: higher-order graph neural networks. In: Proceedings of the AAAI Conference on Artificial Intelligence, vol. 33, pp. 4602–4609 (2019)
14. Putri, W.C., Muscatello, D.J., Stockwell, M.S., Newall, A.T.: Economic burden of seasonal influenza in the United States. Vaccine, **36**(27) (2018)
15. Vanhems, P., et al.: Estimating potential infection transmission routes in hospital wards using wearable proximity sensors. PloS One **8**, 73970 (2013)

Impact of Meta-roles on the Evolution of Organisational Institutions

Amir Hosein Afshar Sedigh[1]([⊠]), Martin K. Purvis[1],
Bastin Tony Roy Savarimuthu[1], Maryam A. Purvis[1],
and Christopher K. Frantz[2]

[1] Department of Information Science, University of Otago, Dunedin, New Zealand
amir.afshar@postgrad.otago.ac.nz,
{martin.purvis,tony.savarimuthu,maryam.purvis}@otago.ac.nz
[2] Department of Computer Science, Norwegian University of Science
and Technology, A205 Ametyst-bygget, Gjøvik, Norway
christopher.frantz@ntnu.no

Abstract. This paper investigates the impact of changes in agents' beliefs coupled with dynamics in agents' meta-roles on the evolution of institutions. The study embeds agents' meta-roles in the BDI architecture. In this context, the study scrutinises the impact of cognitive dissonance in agents due to unfairness of institutions. To showcase our model, two historical long-distance trading societies, namely Armenian merchants of New-Julfa and the English East India Company are simulated. Results show how change in roles of agents coupled with specific institutional characteristics leads to changes of the rules in the system.

Keywords: Institutions · BDI · Agent-based simulation · Meta-roles · Cognitive dissonance

1 Introduction

Employing evolutionary methods to study economic change has attracted several scholars. For instance, Nelson and Winter proposed the idea that "organisational routines" are pivotal in the evolution of business firms (i.e. their role is similar to the role of the genes in biological evolution) [28]. Also, they suggested that "[metaphorically] [r]outines are the skills of an organisation". However, different scholars suggested various definitions of routines. For instance, Feldman and Pentland called "a repetitive, recognizable pattern of interdependent actions, involving multiple actors", a routine [16]. Routines have similarities with institutions (e.g. 'the rules of the game' [25]), in terms of their collective attributes [8] (i.e. they have rule-like conditions [23]). However, whether routines are subconsciously followed (they are simple rules) or they are open to amendments and changes (they are ambiguous rules) is subject of controversy [7]. Hodgson [23] criticised Nelson and Winter's [28] method and pointed to some shortcomings such as not considering 'birth' and 'death' in their method.

© Springer Nature Switzerland AG 2021
S. Swarup and B. T. R. Savarimuthu (Eds.): MABS 2020, LNAI 12316, pp. 66–80, 2021.
https://doi.org/10.1007/978-3-030-66888-4_6

Also, in computer science, role/meta-role based frameworks were developed to facilitate modelling. For instance, Riehle and Gross [29] developed a role modelling approach 'to describe the complexity of object collaborations.' Also, MetaRole-Based Modelling Language (RBML) was expressed in the Unified Modeling Language (UML) to describe patterns' attributes [18]. The CKSW (*Commander–textitKnowledge–Skills–Worker*) framework was proposed for meta-role modelling in agent-based simulation [27]. The idea of integrating roles and institutions is already studied in the context of multi-agent systems. For instance, nested ADICO refined Ostrom's grammar of institutions [13] by differentiating between roles (e.g. enforcer and monitoring agent) [19].

The BDI (beliefs-desires-intention) model is a cognitive agent architecture [9] with some extensions, including the BOID [10], EBDI [26] and the BRIDGE [14] models. This architecture was employed to model agents' cooperation in institutionalised multi-agent systems [5,6].

In light of earlier studies, this paper integrates agents' meta-roles [27] in the BDI architecture and also employs the theory of planned behaviour TPB [17] to model different facets of beliefs. The integrated model is used to investigate how dynamics in agents' meta-roles may lead to the evolution of organisational institutions. Meta-roles in this work are modelled using the CKSW framework that helps modellers to decompose agents in a society based on the characteristics of their roles [27]. The coupling of the CKSW framework within a BDI architecture is investigated in the context of rule-making and -following (how rules are established, interpreted, and followed).

2   An Overview of the Extended BDI Architecture

This extended BDI cognitive architecture is shown in Fig. 1. It can be observed that there are two separate blocks, a left block called '*Events*' and a right block called 'Cognitive architecture'. The Events block represents the events an agent perceives from the environment (e.g. information collected from peers). The *Cognitive architecture* block represents an agent's cognitive decision-making components. Note that when an action is performed by an agent, it will be an input event for those agents interested in that event in the next iteration. A brief description of the four high-level components is provided below. It should be noted that the main focus of this paper is on the addition of *Role* component to the BDI architecture (highlighted in Fig. 1).

- **Roles:** An agent has a set of roles in society regarding established institutions (e.g. agents make those institutions or they monitor their implementations). An agent's role impacts its beliefs, based on individual and social experiences (e.g. it personally may find the rule unfair). We discuss this module in more detail in Sect. 3.
- **Beliefs:** To model beliefs, we are inspired by the idea of different belief components of TPB [17]. This component indicates an agent's perception about the rule and the support the rule has. In other words, an agent has its own

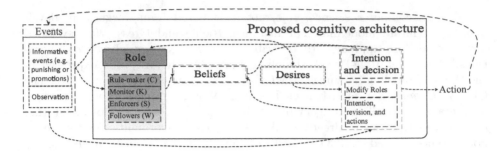

Fig. 1. Proposed cognitive architecture for this model.

internal belief about the rule, and also the perception about the social support for that rule (e.g. rebuking the rule), and an estimation of what an organisation meant by the rule (e.g. consequences of minor violation).
- **Desires:** Agents have different desires, such as an agent's goals and ideal preferences.
- **Intentions and decision:** An agent's intentions for an action and its decision about the final action is formed in this module. The decision results in an action which can be a modification of beliefs and roles or only performing a task.

3   Meta-roles and Role Dynamics

To model agents' roles and their interactions we use CKSW meta-roles [27]. Note that CKSW is a generic model and since this paper concerns the rule-making and rule-following context, we reinterpret those roles in this context as follows:

- *Commander* (**C**): This role is empowered with ultimate authority [27]. In this context, they are the agents who are permitted to *make or revise rules*.
- *Knowledge* (**K**): This role concerns the *know-what* aspect of a society [27]. In this context, these are agents who *monitor and report* the *suspicious activities* of others.
- *Skills* (**S**): This role concerns agents who are known for their skills in society (*know-how*). Unlike knowledge, skills are difficult to communicate and much more so to apply [27]. In the rules context, those agents that have the skills to interpret the rules judge reported agents' activities.
- *Worker* (**W**): These agents perform basic jobs that do not require specialist skills [27]. In this context, they are agents who do not formally collaborate in monitoring, establishing, or interpreting the rules (i.e. the rest of agents).

We also consider two categories of roles, *formal roles* and *informal roles*:

- Formal roles: these roles are defined based on the agent's position in an organisation (one of CKSW meta-roles).

– Informal (internalised) roles: these roles are unofficially and self-assigned (e.g. based on values) by agents such as monitoring, and reporting suspicious behaviours of other agents to managers. These are the role (s) that an agent may perform in addition to its formal role (one or more out of the CKSW meta-roles).

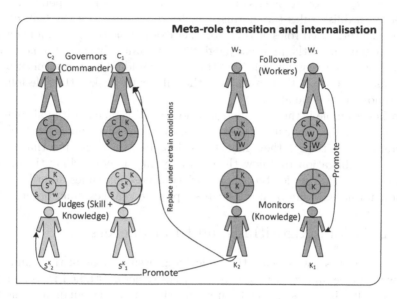

Fig. 2. Transition of formal meta-roles and internalising informal meta-roles—the circles indicate roles that an agent really performs (including internalised roles), and the bigger fonts indicate more involvement in such a role. The arrows indicate the possible transitions in a society.

Figure 2 depicts how an agent's meta-role may evolve[1]. In this example, a worker (say clerk) of an organisation may be promoted to a higher rank after demonstrating competence for such a promotion (say to a manager, a knowledge-based role). If the manager has relevant education, skills and experience, it can be promoted to an even higher position. In these positions, the manager may be responsible for interpreting the situation and deciding about who to fire or hire (i.e. promotion from Knowledge role to the role of a judge (skill)—represented as S^K in the figure). Under certain conditions an agent (Knowledge or Skill) can be promoted to director role (i.e. to the Commander). Note that judges (highlighted in blue) might not be explicitly present on an organisational level for various reasons (e.g. sometimes legal cases go to international courts).

In Fig. 2, the initials for formal roles are indicated on top or bottom of each agent (e.g. K_1) and the list of all roles for an agent (i.e. informal and formal roles)

---

[1] Note that most times agents are downgraded for economic issues or bad performance of agents, and this downgrading can be considered as an extension of this model.

are shown in circles placed near the agents. The font sizes of initials inside these circles indicate the involvement level in such a role, with larger fonts involving more involvement. The involvement is influenced by the ability of an agent to perform a role, as well as the perceived importance of performing such roles from an individual agent's perspective. For instance, some worker agents may adopt additional informal roles in a company (e.g., k for agent W_2). Some worker agents may monitor other agents or they may have a charismatic personality and informally establish rules (i.e. norms) which are executed by the help of other agents (see internalised roles of W_1). Another example is the case of a knowledge agent who may adopt the informal judging role voluntarily (note the addition of S to K_2's formal current role K). Note this agent could adopt the monitoring role for various reasons (e.g. to help stabilise the rule or to weaken the rule-following by not reporting the violators).

Another example is the commanders who may also take additional roles such as K and S (e.g. C_1). They may take some informal roles to influence rule change. For instance, even though they may establish a rule, they may feel that they do not have the obligation to follow them and so they may overlook them, hence impacting rule-following for the whole society. These examples described above show how formal and informal roles can shape rule changes in an organisation.

4   Simulation, Algorithms, and Parameters

In this section, first, we discuss the underlying assumptions of this simulation. Then, we provide an overview of two historical societies studied for simulation, namely the English East India Company (EIC) and Armenian merchants of New-Julfa (Julfa). Then we briefly discuss the aspects of these societies that are of interest for us and the simulation procedures used to represent their agents' behaviour in the simulation context.

4.1   Assumptions

In societies, the rules that exist may not be honoured by agents. Although, the agents know the existence of such rules, they don't follow them and the agents justify this behaviour through the resolution of cognitive dissonance. *Cognitive dissonance* is defined as tensions formed by conflicts between different cognitions (for instance, one likes to smoke, but loathes to get cancer) [3]. These tensions lead to creating some justification for taking one action (quit smoking or continuing). This idea was used to attribute workers' productivity to cognitive dissonance regarding fairness of institutions [2]. In particular, studies showed that procedural justice (having fair dispute resolution mechanisms) increases public law obedience and cooperation with the police [32]. Also, underpaid or overpaid persons alter their efforts put forth on the system (e.g. efforts or voluntarily performed tasks) to make the system fairer for themselves [1]. In this work, we consider that agents justify the need for rule change (or don't follow rules), because they need to resolve this cognitive dissonance (i.e. they justify not following rules, or the reason to keep following the rules).

4.2   Societies

As stated earlier, in this paper, we investigate two long-distance trading societies, namely Armenian merchants of New-Julfa (Julfa) and the East India Company (EIC). The two societies were contemporaneous and shared the same areas for trading products (e.g. the EIC managers granted Julfans permissions for using the EIC infrastructures [4]). Also, both societies faced principal-agent problem [24]—the dilemma where the self-interested decisions of a party (agent) impact the benefits of the other person on whose behalf these decisions are made (principal).

Armenian Merchants of New-Julfa (Julfa): Armenian merchants of New-Julfa were originally from old Julfa in Armenia. They re-established a trader society in New-Julfa (near Isfahan, Iran) after their forced displacement in the early 17th century [4,22]. They used commenda contracts (profit-sharing contracts) in the society and also used courts to resolve disputes [4,22].

The English East India Company (EIC): During the same time, the EIC (AD 1600s–1850s) had a totally different perspective on managing the society. The EIC faced a high mortality rate due to environmental factors in India. EIC paid fixed wages and fired agents based on their own beliefs about their trading behaviour. Furthermore, EIC's trading period covers the English Civil War (1642–1651), which led to inclusion of some of the senior mangers on the board of directors and granting permission for private trade to the employees (i.e. trading activities for individuals' self-interests).

In both of these societies agents' meta-roles changed over time. More precisely in EIC, a mercantile or trader agent (W) after gaining experience was promoted to a managerial position to monitor other mercantile agents (K). Also, in EIC, after the English Civil War, managers had the opportunity to be part of the board of directors (C). In Julfa, the promotions took place based on the ageing of the family members (i.e. agents got promoted from one meta-role to the other gradually). Additionally, in Julfa mercantile agents (W) and heads of families (C) formed the courts (S). In this model, we use the EIC dynamics in organisational meta-roles (i.e. promotion of agents) to make the two systems comparable. Note that this change in dynamics decreases the opportunities for Julfans to revise their rules. However, we know that the rules were deeply honoured by Julfans [4].

Environment: These societies had different mortality rates. On average an EIC agent died before the age of 35 due to harsh environmental circumstances [20]. Julfan traders did not face such a situation [4] and the closed trading society of Julfa would have collapsed under a high mortality rate [30].

Fairness: Another difference between the two historical long-distance trading societies is associated with their payment schemes for employees and the adjudication processes (i.e. use of courts for resolving disputes about suspicious behaviour). EIC rarely employed an adjudication process (e.g. agents were fired based on their performance because of suspected cheating), and the agents were paid low wages [21]. However, in Julfa a mercantile agent was paid based on his performance [4]. Julfans had adjudication processes to resolve disputes, which considered available evidence [4]. Though Julfa appears to be fairer than EIC in terms of payment, total fairness can be questioned—for instance, in the Julfa society, the family wealth and trade was managed and controlled by the eldest brother [22]. This rule deprived younger ones from managing their own share of capital.

4.3   Algorithms

In this subsection, we discuss the procedures employed to simulate role changes within the two societies. The simulation model is split into four distinctive procedures. The first procedure models the societal level of simulation, including creating an initial population and staffing (hiring new mercantile agents) to create a stable population. The second level describes procedures for *mercantile agents'* (W) decision-making and learning the system's parameters. The third level covers the decision-making and learning procedure associated with managers (K). The last procedure is the meta-algorithm that sequentially executes the aforementioned algorithms and updates appropriate parameters. In this algorithm, agent meta-roles may change and the opportunity for institutional dynamics is provided (i.e., promotion of K agents to C and changes in institutions).

Algorithm 1: Societal level set-up and initialisation

/* Intialise the system starting with *iteration* $\leftarrow$ 0.   */
1 Create 500 new agents with *status* $\leftarrow$ *new*, random personality aspects, and random parameters
2 Assign appropriate roles (i.e. mercantile, managers, and directors) to created agents
/* n = deceased and fired agents (mercantile agents and managers) in the previous iteration.   */
3 The most experienced mercantile agents get promoted to a managerial role
4 Create n new agents with: *status* $\leftarrow$ *new*, *Experiene* $\leftarrow$ 0, and randomly initialise parameters
/* Perceived environment and fairness for inexperienced agents.   */
5 $PEnvironment \leftarrow RandomUniform(0, 1)$
6 $Fair \leftarrow RandomUniform(0, 1)$

Algorithm 1 shows how the societal level of the system is simulated. In iteration 0, the system is initialised by creating 500 new agents with random parameters (line 1). The roles are assigned to created agents (about 2% directors, 5% managers, and the rest mercantile agents).[2] The organisation hires and promotes agents to sustain the number of agents per role—i.e. replaces deceased agents (lines 3–4). The rest of the algorithm is executed only for inexperienced agents (i.e. new recruits). An agent has a completely random understanding of the system's characteristics (lines 5–6).

---

[2] These numbers are inspired from the numbers in the EIC [20].

Algorithm 2: Mercantile agent's algorithm (for meta-role W)

```
   /* Update parameters for new recruits.                              */
 1 if Status = New then Set agent's parameter using Algorithm. 1
 2 if Experience > 3 then
       /* Update role and the decision to perform private trade.       */
 3     if Dissonance(Fair) < DissonThresh then
           /* Agent stops monitoring violations.                       */
 4         Remove K from voluntarily performed roles
 5         if ((Fair < thresh) or
               (No. PrivateTraderFriends / No. Friends < JustifThresh)) then
               /* Agent decides to perform private trade.              */
 6             PrivateTrade ← OK
 7         end
 8     end
       /* Agent voluntarily collaborates in monitoring.                */
 9     if Dissonance(Fair) > DissonThresh then  Voluntarily perform K
10 end
   /* learning;                                                        */
11 if Experience > 3 then
       /* Reporting observed violations;                               */
12     if Voluntarily performing K then
           /* The agent reports some of the cheaters observed.         */
13         Agent reports connections who impose more costs on the organisation
           than his tolerance (internalised S).
14     end
15 end
16 Learn parameters and adjust the beliefs about rules
17 Experience ← Experience + 1
18 if Rand(1) ≤ MortalityProbability(Experience + 15) then Die
```

Algorithm 2 shows the procedure associated with mercantile agents' decision-making process. Note that in this algorithm $\#Rnd(x)$ indicates a random number generated in the interval $(0, x)$. As stated earlier, if the status of the mercantile agent is new, he goes through an initialisation (see Algorithm 1, lines 3–4). Furthermore, experienced mercantile agents decide on their participation in monitoring by considering cognitive dissonance incurred (based on their perception of institutional fairness and dissonance toleration). They also decide on performing private trade with respect to the perceived fairness and their friends who perform such trades (lines 3–7). If the mercantile agent has enough experience and has already decided to collaborate in monitoring, he helps the system to identify violators, based on his interpretation of a fair action (lines 8–9). Finally, the mercantile agent updates his perception of system parameters (e.g. fairness of the society), increases his experience, and may die (lines 10–12).

Algorithm 3 shows the procedures associated with managers (i.e. monitoring agents (K)). A manager creates a set that consists of reported violators with unacceptable violations (i.e. he tolerates violations to some extent, see line 1).

Algorithm 3: Manager's algorithm (for meta-role K)

```
/* Manager reports (and eventually punishes) a number of employees
   who violate the rules of the organisation beyond its tolerance
   level. We call the threshold TolPunish.                        */
```
1 $PotPunish \leftarrow$ employees with violations more than $TolPunish$
2 **if** *The number of members of PotPunish* $> MaxPunish$ **then**
```
    /* The manager has a limit for the number of agents he can punish
       called MaxPunish.                                          */
```
3 $\quad$ Punish $MaxPunish$ out of $PotPunish$ that have the most violation
4 **else**
5 $\quad$ Punish all $PotPunish$ members.
6 **end**
7 $Experience \leftarrow Experience + 1$
8 **if** $Rand(1) \leq MortalityProbability(Experience + 15)$ **then** Die

---

Note that the manager reports about the violators and punishes a certain number. If the number of violators exceeds a certain threshold, he punishes the worst violators (lines 2–3). Otherwise, all the violators are punished (lines 4–5). Finally, the agent's experience and age increase, and the agent may die (lines 6–7).

Algorithm 4: Meta algorithm

```
/* Intialise the system starting with iteration ← 0.            */
```
1 Create 500 new agents with $status \leftarrow new$ and random parameters with appropriate roles
```
/* Call algorithms in an appropriate sequence.                  */
```
2 **repeat**
3 $\quad$ Run Algorithm 1
4 $\quad$ Run Algorithm 2
5 $\quad$ Run Algorithm 3
6 $\quad$ **if** $iteration = 70$ **then**
7 $\quad\quad$ Update board of directors (C) with new managers
8 $\quad\quad$ **if** *majority support private trade* **then** legalise private trade and reduce wages
9 $\quad$ **end**
10 $\quad$ $iteration \leftarrow iteration + 1$
11 **until** $iteration = 250$

Algorithm 4 is the main algorithm that calls the other procedures. In iteration 0, the system is initialised by creating 500 new agents with random parameters. The roles are assigned to created agents (2% directors (C), 5% managers (K), and the rest are mercantile agents (W)), and they have 0 years of experience (line 1). Then, 250 iterations corresponding to 250 years, containing specific steps (lines 3–9) are performed (250). The first step is to run the societal algorithm (i.e. Algorithm 1, line 3). Then the algorithm associated with the mercantile agents is run (i.e. Algorithm 2). Finally, the manager's decisions are made using Algorithm 3 (line 5). When the simulation reaches the year that some of the managers in the EIC (who started as mercantile agents) are promoted to the board of directors (i.e. consequences of the English Civil War, iteration 70), a decision about permitting (or legalising) private trade is made (lines 6–8).

4.4 Parameters

In this subsection, we discuss the important parameters employed in the simulation (see Table 1), along with the reasons for choosing specific values for them. Note that we used 250 iterations to reflect the longevity of EIC (it was active with some interruptions and changes in power from 1600 to 1850). In Table 1, column 'Name' indicates the names of parameters, column 'Comment' shows additional information if required, column 'Distribution' indicates the probability distribution used for these parameters, and column 'Values' indicates the values of parameters estimated for the two societies. Note that these parameters can be modified to reflect other societies.

Table 1. Parameters associated with the model

Variable name	Comment	Distribution	Values
Fairness	Unfair: Fair	Constant	$-0.4 : 0.6$
Perception of environment and fairness of system		Uniform	$(-1, 1)$
Thresholds	Dissonance Environment Fired agents	Uniform	$(0, 1)$ $(0, 1)$ $(0, 0.3)$
Monitoring	Boolean	Bernoulli	0.5
Permission for private trade	Percent of joined managers who agreed to change	Constant	70%

Fairness: Note that as discussed earlier, Julfa had fairer institutions than the EIC. We set system fairness values to 0.6 and −0.4 for fair and unfair societies respectively. We believe that neither of these two societies were totally fair or unfair (e.g. EIC managers justified the firing of agents that indicates there has some effort towards fairness).

Perceived Characteristics: Because of lack of prior experience, the new agents have a totally random understanding of social characteristics.

Thresholds: These are the numbers that reflect an agent's tolerance of different aspects and characteristics of the system. All these thresholds are generated at random except for firing. For the proportion of fired agents, we assume that a manager would fire 30% of the suspected employees.

Monitoring: In the model, a recruit may voluntarily decide to participate in monitoring—we use a random boolean generator to represent this.

Permission for Private Trade: In this simulation, we assume that permission is granted if more than 70% in the board of directors agree to such a decision (i.e. 8 out of 11).

Furthermore, we parametrise the agents' learning as follows. Agents discount information using a weight of 30% for the past. This reflects the importance of recent information for agents.

5   Results

In this section, we describe the simulation results considering *four* different combinations of two characteristics, namely a) environmental circumstances and b) fairness of institutions. With two different values for each of these characteristics, four combinations are possible (see Table 2).

Table 2. System specification based on different characteristics

Characteristics	E_0F_0 (EIC)	E_0F_1	E_1F_0	E_1F_1 (Julfa)
Environment	✗	✗	✓	✓
Fairness	✗	✓	✗	✓

The configurations (i.e., societies) are identified by the first letter of the characteristics, namely E and F that are representatives of the environmental characteristic of (E) and fairness of the institutions (F), respectively. A tick indicates that the society possesses such an attribute, and a cross indicates the society does not possess such an attribute. In this table, we gradually change characteristics of the EIC (E_0F_0) to get closer to Julfa (E_1F_1), to examine their effects on the success of these societies. We utilised *NetLogo* to perform our simulations [33]. We also used 30 different runs for each set-up and then averaged their results. Finally, note that the patterns observed in simulation results are compared to the patterns reported from the EIC and Jufla, because we had access to the qualitative data.

5.1   Permissions for Private Trade

Table 3 presents the percentage of simulation runs (out of 30) where the permission for private trade was granted (see row "Permission granted"). Note that this change in rule (granting of permission) happened due to changes in agents' meta-roles where a mercantile agent progresses to the board of directors (and advocates the decision to permit private trade). As can be seen from the results, both unfair societies (F_0) had higher percentage of runs where the private trade is permitted (>50%), although with a large difference (93% and 57% respectively). In fair societies, none of the runs resulted in private trade being approved. This result mirrors the evidence from Julfa. In Julfa, mercantile agents (W) and peripheral managers (K) were the ones who eventually ran the family business (C). Also, mercantile agents and managers made decisions regarding violations and acted as juries in certain courts [4]. The aforementioned situation, combined with keeping private trade illegal [22], indicate that this rule was socially accepted[3]. Also, we know that in the EIC, the permission for private trade was granted once the managers had the opportunity to be part of the board of directors [15].

Table 3. Percentage of runs where private trade was permitted (out of 30 runs).

Societies	Permission granted for private trade
$E_0 F_0$ (EIC)	93%
$E_0 F_1$	0%
$E_1 F_0$	57%
$E_1 F_1$ (Julfa)	0%

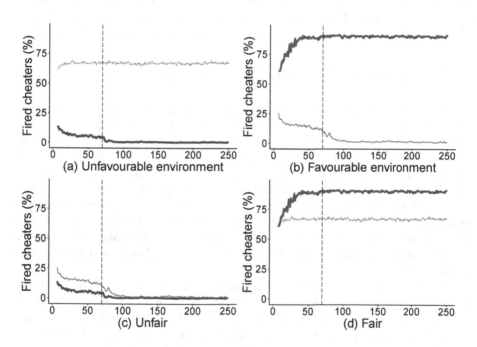

Fig. 3. Monitoring strength and firing in simulated societies.

---

[3] Because in none of the simulation runs of Julfa the permission was granted, we believe that using a similar dynamics to Julfa would not change the results.

5.2   Fired Violators (Monitoring Strength)

Now we discuss the impact of aforementioned two characteristics on the monitoring strength of the system (see Fig. 3). Figures 3a–3d present the percentage of the cheating agents fired. In these figures, the y-axis indicates the percentage of fired cheaters. As can be seen, the most fired agents belong to society E_1F_1 and then E_0F_1. These indicate the importance of fairness of institutions on the system's monitoring strength.

This impact that we see in Fig. 3 is a consequence of two informal roles performed by agents, namely a) mercantile agents (W) that monitor and report suspicious behaviours (internalised K) to managers (formal K), and b) managers (K) who interpret rules based on the situations and tolerate some behaviours (S). For example, managers who think the system isn't fair, may not report the cheating behaviour of agents (agents who are involved in private trades). And these same managers who become a part of the board of directors allow for these private trades to happen legally (but with the reduction in wages further, though). Also, in organisations with unfair institutions, after granting permissions for private trade (year 70), agents' collaboration in monitoring the cheaters (for theft etc.) decreases. Note that the evidence for interpretation of the rules can be found in EIC managers' correspondence[4]. Also, these results mirror the evidence of rare cheating and successful monitoring mechanisms in Julfa [4] and the popularity of cheating and collusion in the EIC [11].

6   Discussion and Concluding Remarks

This study has presented an extension of the BDI cognitive architecture to investigate its interaction with agents meta-roles. Also, using this extension, the study has investigated the impact of a combination of a) dynamics in agents' roles and b) the institutional characteristics (i.e. mortality rate and fairness) on organisational rule dynamics (i.e. change of rule). As the role of individuals changes (e.g. W to K), their beliefs formed based in their previous role impacts their new decisions. Finally, our study has used the evidence from empirical studies to simulate two historical long-distance trading societies, namely Armenian merchants of new Julfa (Julfa) and the English East India Company (EIC) and has demonstrated what may cause rule changes (i.e. role change and institutional characteristics).

The simulation results mirrored historical evidence. It has shown that the fairness of institutions is a pivotal characteristic to drive their stability (i.e. avoiding revisions in rules) and in facilitating agents' collaboration in monitoring each other's behaviours. These results (i.e. changes in rules and weak monitoring and reporting) mirror concerns in the modern context about the division of "rules into the two categories of rules-in-use and rules-in-form" [31]. For instance, it is

---

[4] For instance, in the early years, some managers defended mercantile agents' private trade by stating: "if some tolleration [sic] for private trade be not permitted none but desperate men will sail our ships" [11].

noted that rules-in-use (followed rules) in some provinces of Canada might have been rules-in-forms (unfollowed rules that do not have any effect on behaviour) in others [31]. There exist some obstacles in a law in becoming a rule-in-use [12]. An instance of this obstacle is the activities of monitoring agents who interpret the law differently and thus hamper its effectiveness (e.g. through not monitoring violations) and hence can aid the formation of new rules similar to what has been observed in results from Table 3 and Fig. 3.

A future extension of the study, will involve detailed examination of the interaction between other modules of the cognitive architecture presented in Fig. 1. Also, the simulation can be extended to take account of other characteristics of these historical societies, such as the personalities of agents, to provide a more fine-grained model.

References

1. Adams, J.S.: Inequity in social exchange. Adv. Exp. Soc. Psychol. **2**, 267–299 (1965)
2. Adams, J.S., Rosenbaum, W.B.: The relationship of worker productivity to cognitive dissonance about wage inequities. J. Appl. Psychol. **46**(3), 161–164 (1962)
3. Aronson, E., Aronson, J.: The Social Animal, 10th edn. Worth Pub, NY (2007)
4. Aslanian, S.D.: From the Indian Ocean to the Mediterranean: Circulation and the global trade networks of Armenian merchants from New Julfa/Isfahan, 1605–1747. Phd thesis, Columbia University, NY (2007)
5. Balke, T., De Vos, M., Padget, J., Traskas, D.: On-line reasoning for institutionally-situated bdi agents. In: The 10th International Conference on Autonomous Agents and Multiagent Systems. AAMAS 2011, International Foundation for Autonomous Agents and Multiagent Systems, Richland, SC, vol. 3, pp. 1109–1110 (2011)
6. Balke, T., De Vos, M., Padget, J.: Normative run-time reasoning for institutionally-situated BDI agents. In: Cranefield, S., van Riemsdijk, M.B., Vázquez-Salceda, J., Noriega, P. (eds.) COIN -2011. LNCS (LNAI), vol. 7254, pp. 129–148. Springer, Heidelberg (2012). https://doi.org/10.1007/978-3-642-35545-5_8
7. Becker, M.C.: Organizational routines: a review of the literature. Ind. Corp. Change **13**(4), 643–678 (2004). https://doi.org/10.1093/icc/dth026
8. Becker, M.C.: Handbook of organizational routines, chap. The past, present and future of organizational routines: introduction to the Handbook of Organizational Routines, first edn. pp. 3–14. Edward Elgar, MA, USA (2008)
9. Bratman, M.E., Israel, D.J., Pollack, M.E.: Plans and resource-bounded practical reasoning. Comput. Intell. **4**(3), 349–355 (1988)
10. Broersen, J., Dastani, M., Hulstijn, J., Huang, Z., van der Torre, L.: The boid architecture: conflicts between beliefs, obligations, intentions and desires. In: Proceedings of AGENTS, NY, pp. 9–16. ACM (2001)
11. Chaudhuri, K.N.: The English East India Company: The Study of an Early Joint-Stock company 1600–1640, 1st edn. Frank Cass & Co., Ltd., London, UK (1965)
12. Cole, D.H.: Laws, norms, and the institutional analysis and development framework. J. Inst. Econ. **13**(4), 829–847 (2017)
13. Crawford, S.E.S., Ostrom, E.: A grammar of institutions. Am. Political Sci. Rev. **89**(3), 582–600 (1995). https://doi.org/10.2307/2082975

14. Dignum, F., Dignum, V., Jonker, C.M.: Towards agents for policy making. In: David, N., Sichman, J.S. (eds.) MABS 2008. LNCS (LNAI), vol. 5269, pp. 141–153. Springer, Heidelberg (2009). https://doi.org/10.1007/978-3-642-01991-3_11

15. Erikson, E.: Between Monopoly and Free Trade: The English East India Company, 1600–1757, 1st edn. Princeton Univ. Press, NJ (2014)

16. Feldman, M.S., Pentland, B.T.: Reconceptualizing organizational routines as a source of flexibility and change. Administrative Sci. Q. 48(1), 94 (2003). https://doi.org/10.2307/355662010.2307/3556620

17. Fishbein, M., Ajzen, I.: Predicting and Changing Behavior: The Reasoned Action Approach, 1st edn. Psychology Press Ltd., NY (2011)

18. France, R., Kim, D., Song, E., Ghosh, S.: Metarole-based modeling language (RBML) specification V1.0. Technical Report, Computer Science Department, Colorado State University, CO, USA (2002)

19. Frantz, C., Purvis, M.K., Nowostawski, M., Savarimuthu, B.T.R.: nADICO: a nested grammar of institutions. In: Boella, G., Elkind, E., Savarimuthu, B.T.R., Dignum, F., Purvis, M.K. (eds.) PRIMA 2013. LNCS (LNAI), vol. 8291, pp. 429–436. Springer, Heidelberg (2013). https://doi.org/10.1007/978-3-642-44927-7_31

20. Hejeebu, S.: Microeconomic investigations of the English East India Company. Phd thesis, University of Iowa, Iowa, January 1998

21. Hejeebu, S.: Contract enforcement in the English East India company. J. Econ. Hist. 65(2), 496–523 (2005)

22. Herzig, E.M.: The Armenian merchants of New Julfa, Isfahan: A study in premodern Asian trade. Phd thesis, Oxford University, Oxford, UK (1991)

23. Hodgson, G.M.: The mystery of the routine. Revue économique 54(2), 355–384 (2003). https://doi.org/10.3917/reco.542.0355

24. Mitnick, B.M.: Origin of the theory of agency: an account by one of the theory's originators. SSRN Electron. J. (2011). https://doi.org/10.2139/ssrn.1020378

25. North, D.C.: Institutions. J. Econ. Perspect. 5(1), 97–112 (1991). https://doi.org/10.1257/jep.5.1.97

26. Pereira, D., Oliveira, E., Moreira, N.: Formal modelling of emotions in BDI agents. In: Sadri, F., Satoh, K. (eds.) CLIMA 2007. LNCS (LNAI), vol. 5056, pp. 62–81. Springer, Heidelberg (2008). https://doi.org/10.1007/978-3-540-88833-8_4

27. Purvis, M.K., Purvis, M.A., Frantz, C.K.: CKSW: a folk-sociological meta-model for agent-based modelling. In: Social Path Workshop. University of Surrey (2014)

28. Nelson, R.R., Winter, S.G.: An Evolutionary Theory of Economic Change, 1st edn. Harvard University Press, Cambridge, Massachusetts, United States (1982)

29. Riehle, D., Gross, T.: Role model based framework design and integration. In: Proceedings of the 13th ACM SIGPLAN Conference on Object-oriented Programming, Systems, Languages, and Applications - OOPSLA 1998. ACM Press (1998)

30. Sedigh, A.H.A., Frantz, C.K., Savarimuthu, B.T.R., Purvis, M.K., Purvis, M.A.: A comparison of two historical trader societies – an agent-based simulation study of English East India company and New-Julfa. In: Davidsson, P., Verhagen, H. (eds.) MABS 2018. LNCS (LNAI), vol. 11463, pp. 17–31. Springer, Cham (2019). https://doi.org/10.1007/978-3-030-22270-3_2

31. Sproule-Jones, M.: Governments at Work: Canadian Parliamentary Federalism and its Public Policy Effects, 1st edn. Univ. of Toronto Press, Toronto (1993)

32. Sunshine, J., Tyler, T.R.: The role of procedural justice and legitimacy in shaping public support for policing. Law Soc. Rev. 37(3), 513–548 (2003)

33. Wilensky, U.: Netlogo. Center for Connected Learning and Computer-Based Modeling, Northwestern University, Evanston, IL, Technical Report (1999)

Optimization of Large-Scale Agent-Based Simulations Through Automated Abstraction and Simplification

Alexey Tregubov[✉] and Jim Blythe

USC Information Sciences Institute, Marina Del Rey, CA, USA
{tregubov,blythe}@isi.edu

Abstract. Agent-based simulations of social media platforms often need to be run for many repetitions at large scale. Often, researchers must compromise between available computational resources (memory, run-time), the scale of the simulation, and the quality of its predictions.

As a step to support this process, we present a systematic exploration of simplifications of agent simulations across a number of dimensions suitable for social media studies. Simplifications explored include sub-sampling, implementing agents representing teams or groups of users, simplifying agent behavior, and simplifying the environment.

We also propose a tool that helps apply simplifications to a simulation model, and helps find simplifications that approximate the behavior of the full-scale simulation within computational resource limits.

We present experiments in two social media domains, GitHub and Twitter, using data both to design agents and to test simulation predictions against ground truth. Sub-sampling agents often provides a simple and effective strategy in these domains, particularly in combination with simplifying agent behavior, yielding up to an order of magnitude improvement in run-time with little or no loss in predictive power. Moreover, some simplifications improve performance over the full-scale simulation by removing noise.

We describe domain characteristics that may indicate the most effective simplification strategies and discuss heuristics for automatic exploration of simplifications.

Keywords: Abstractions · Simplifications · Agent-based simulation · Massive scale simulations · Online social networks

1 Motivation

Large-scale simulations may be used for many purposes, including prediction and exploration of what-if scenarios. Typically, a large number of parameters, such as behavioral characteristics of individual agents, may not be known precisely but are modeled probabilistically, requiring many iterations of the simulation as parameters are varied systematically to arrive at an estimate that is accurate

© Springer Nature Switzerland AG 2021
S. Swarup and B. T. R. Savarimuthu (Eds.): MABS 2020, LNAI 12316, pp. 81–93, 2021.
https://doi.org/10.1007/978-3-030-66888-4_7

and whose dependence on the parameter space is known. This can be a very expensive process.

A common solution is to iterate and test over smaller, simpler versions of the problem that are chosen to provide a close estimate to the simulation outcomes under test while requiring considerably less run-time and memory to run. In some cases, the final estimate may be more precise although each individual run may be less so, because many more iterations are possible. The simplifications used are typically drawn from a standard set of broad categories including (1) reducing the number of agents and considering a sub-region of the original simulation, (2) simplifying the agent decision processes to use less computation and memory, (3) simplifying the representation of the environment, (4) selectively replacing subsets of either the agents, the environment or both with direct models of the behavior of a group of agents or region of the environment, and (5) simplifying and/or reducing the communication that takes place between agents, which often dominates the computational complexity of a simulation. Domain-dependent simplifications, for example based on geographic constraints of agents, may combine several of these categories. Often, developers follow an ad hoc process: while the simulation may be simplified in many ways, only one or two are typically used, without evidence for which simplification may yield the best estimates of the parameters to optimize the full-scale simulation. While transformations may be required in order to adapt the results from the abstract problem into the full-scale problem, they are typically not explored in detail.

In this paper we take a first step towards an empirically-based tool for selecting an appropriate simplification from a rich set of possible approaches in a realistic domain. While other work, described below, has used formal methods to show that an abstraction will provide the correct result and is as simple as possible, the empirical approach we propose can be applied to large simulations that may require the use of code that is not sufficiently modeled to support a formal approach. We define a number of ways in which a multi-agent simulation may be simplified, and for each one we discuss the kinds of information about the full-scale simulation that may be most faithfully estimated by this simplification. We investigate a number of simplifications in the context of two domains: a massive simulation of GitHub users, with trace data describing around 10 million users and 30 million repositories, and a large simulation of Twitter containing 650 k users and 1.6 million tweets. We introduce a full-scale simulation to predict the next two months of activity on GitHub or Twitter based on four months of trace data, in which each agent is described by statistics on their past history and a set of parameters describing how future behavior may be produced based on the history. Next, we explore a number of abstractions of the full-scale simulation in order to optimize parameters for the agents, and discuss which abstractions combine the most accurate estimates with the greatest savings of computational resources. These abstractions may be used individually or in combination to reduce the computational expense of running a simulation by several orders of magnitude in some cases.

We find that, in a broad range of situations, simple domain-independent modifications such as agent sub-sampling can yield simulations that provide predictions similar to those of the full-scale simulation with a fraction of the time or memory requirements. In other cases, domain-dependent simplifications are required for such improvements, and we show how they can be derived from domain-independent principles, such as reducing the action space of the agents or aggregating agents. In a small but significant number of cases, the reduced simulation yields better prediction results than the full-scale simulation using a fraction of the resources. This happens when the agents, actions or world features removed were predominantly a source of noise for the predictions of interest.

Finally we review other large-scale simulations from the literature to verify that the abstractions we consider make sense within those simulations and may be expected to yield useful results. We also discuss how the framework for abstractions may be used to run simplified simulations in cases where the full-scale simulation is infeasible, and how experiments such as the ones we describe may help indicate the most useful simplifications within a single partially abstracted simulation. This is an active area of investigation within our group.

The novel contributions of this paper include the first comparative, empirical exploration of a broad set of simplification criteria across multiple simulation domains. While previous work, described below, investigated one or more simplifications in a simulation domain, we compare an expanded set of techniques within the same framework and discuss the extent to which they are domain-independent or whether domain dependent modifications may be necessary to apply them. Another contribution is an initial framework to help experimenters to consider a broader set of possible simplifications that lays the groundwork for semi-automated tools to simplify simulations.

2 Related Work

Struss [15] distinguishes abstraction, simplification and approximation in the context of model-based reasoning. In this view, abstraction and approximation are both special cases of simplification, which is a general change to a model, perhaps altering relations between variables describing a problem, that reduces some modeling details. An abstraction is a kind of simplification that proposes a new model, e.g. by changing the set of variables or their domains. An approximation may replace a function in the model with a simpler version, some of whose values differ from the original. Our work broadly follows this categorization. De Kleer [6] and others address the question of finding the appropriate level of abstraction for a problem, defined as the simplest abstract version that is adequate to solve the problem. Here we explore the same issue, but empirically rather than analytically, since elements of a simulation may take the form of complex code for which such reasoning is intractable. In this paper, we use term simplification for all abstractions, simplifications and approximations.

Work on abstractions in planning systems may be viewed as simplifications to the decision space of a single agent or its environment, e.g. [9,10]. This work motivated us to explore reductions in the action space for agents in general simulations. In a similar way, Cohen et al. derive abstractions in multi-agent simulation systems that provably preserve certain temporal properties of the simulation [5].

Simplifications and abstractions were explored in simulation of biochemical systems by Rhodes et al. [13]. To reduce model complexity Rhodes et al. experimented with scale (number of agents), time step, complexity of inter-agent messaging and conflict resolution. Authors used runtime and accuracy as metrics to evaluate the impact of each simplification. They conclude that some simplifications (e.g. number of agents, time step) can be varied significantly to reduce runtime within the reasonable accuracy range. In this paper, in addition to runtime we also explore memory usage and various accuracy metrics for social networks.

Shirazi et al. [14] dynamically replace groups of agents that occupy the same geographical area with a single agent representing the group. This is a spatial version of the general principle of aggregating agents based on shared interaction, which we define below and present a social network-based approach for in Sect. 4.3.

There is a comprehensive body of research on developing domain and application specific abstractions and simplifications [3,8,12,13]. However, finding simplifications and identifying ranges of parameters that produce useful reductions is often a manual process. Automated search is rarely discussed in literature.

3   Simplification Types

In this section we discuss a number of general types of simplification, shown in Table 1. Some of these represent domain-independent simplification methods that can be used in any multi-agent simulation while others are domain-independent principles that may or may not yield domain-dependent methods for a given problem. As we discuss the trade-off of computational resources consumed and accuracy below, we assume that there is some metric that is applied to the simulation, for example it might be used to evaluate which is best of a set of potential policies, or make predictions given some initial conditions. In the absence of ground truth for the metric, we seek a simplification that performs as closely as possible to the full-scale simulation on the metric, although it may behave quite differently on measures that are not of interest to the problem.

3.1   Subsampling

Simulation of the entire population can be computationally expensive. Subsampling identifies a smaller subset of agents and resources with the aim of reproducing the behavior of the entire population in order to meet the original goal of the simulation. Identifying a smaller subset of agents and resources that can reproduce behavior of the entire population may require exploring a wide range of parameters. One approach is to exploit any structure that might be found within the simulation framework, for example:

Table 1. Types of simplifications. Rows correspond to aspects of the simulation to be simplified, while columns denote whether the simplification is a reduction of a group of objects or involves creating a new model.

Target	Reduction	Abstraction
Set of agents	E.g.: Subsampling of agents	E.g.: Aggregate agents into meta-agents
Agents' decision space	E.g.: Reduce action types	E.g.: Aggregate actions
Environment	E.g.: Reduce resources used	E.g.: Aggregate resources,environment data
Set of events	E.g.: Reduce amount of generated events	E.g.: Aggregate events
Agents' communication	E.g.: Frequency of synchronization among agents	

- When simulating a social network one may select a smaller number of agents and associated resources by selecting a small number of connected components.
- For simulations where historical data on agents' activity is available, one can select agents that were active recently, disregarding agents which were not active after some threshold.
- If the environment allows geographical segmentation, running the simulation on a smaller number of segments can reduce the number of agents while preserving local properties.

This class of simplifications may be one of the easiest to apply in a domain-independent way, since it is possible to treat agents and their decisions and communications as black boxes. For example, domain-independent strategies for subsampling include random selection. In this paper we discuss random and frequency-based subsampling of agents, resources and actions/events.

3.2 Simplifying Agents' Decision Process

Each agent's decision process may be complex, possibly depending on many environmental conditions, leading to a heavy computational burden. To reduce runtime we can simplify agents' decision making process. Agents' behavior simplification can be applied to all agents or to just a subset. Making a small simplification in the decision process in a simulation with millions of agents can significantly reduce overall runtime.

There are different ways to approach agents' decision process simplification:

– Approximation of data and parameters needed to make decision. For example, decision process can be approximated with probabilistic models using historical data. This could be precomputed in advance.
– Simplification of decision rules, reducing the number of steps in the process.
– Reducing possible actions in agent's decision process.

Additionally, depending on the process this approach can reduce size of the agent and overall memory requirements. For example, if aggregate measurements and values are no longer needed this memory can be released.

Simpler decision processes tend to require less external data, which makes agents less dependent on the environment. This property is useful when parallel simulation is developed, it simplifies synchronization of the shared environment.

This approach has limitations. Just as small simplifications to each of millions of agents may have a significant impact on runtime and memory usage, small discrepancies in the behavior of each agent may combine to produce significant inaccuracies in metrics applied to the simulation.

This simplification is often domain-dependent since it modifies internal processes of the agent.

3.3 Selectively Replacing Groups of Agents with One Agent

In a large-scale simulation it is often possible to identify classes of agents that share similar properties and behavior. Some of these classes can be modeled as one agent that represents activities of the group as a whole, effectively creating a simulation that combines components modeled at different resolutions.

It is possible to apply simplifications of this type in a domain-independent manner since external features of the agents, such as geographic location or agent type, can be used to form groups while treating the agent as a black box and aggregating the observed actions. However more effective groups tend to be found using domain-dependent methods that can exploit regularities in decision-making, for example, or allow communication to be localized.

3.4 Simplifying Communication Between Agents

In large-scale simulations communication can consume a lot of computational and network capacity. In distributed parallel simulations, this problem is especially acute because of the network limitations.

We note that this is a distinct strategy from optimizing communication in the simulation. In optimization, the same information is shared between agents at the same time as in the original simulation. In simplification, communications may be degraded in content or timing, trading off fidelity of the simulation for memory and run-time reductions. Methods for optimization include caching frequently sent information and using communication hubs to decentralize information distribution. In distributed parallel simulations, one may partition the agents across computational nodes so as to minimize expensive cross-node communications [1].

There are different approaches to simplifying communication among agents:

- Reduced/simplified communication, where messages may be strategically dropped or summarized.
- Bulk information update, in which eventually the same information is communicated, but at any given time an agent may have received less information than in a high-resolution communication environment.

Other simplifications can also help to reduce resource consumption (e.g. memory) and allow researchers to use fewer compute nodes or in some cases avoid parallel computations altogether. Reducing the number of communicating compute nodes reduces communication overhead among agents and the environment. This simplification is often used in combination with others.

This simplification is often domain-dependent, because it requires knowledge of the environment and agents' communication protocols.

4   Experiments

4.1   Simplifications Support in FARM

FARM is an agent-based simulation framework with support for large-scale simulations. It is implemented in Python. FARM architecture provides components to model social networks [1–3]. We conducted our experiments with simplifications using FARM. FARM supports some of the simplification operators for simulation models described above. It also implements a simple search for operator parameters that yield a compromise between runtime and memory and a quality metric of the simulation.

4.2   GitHub and Twitter Simulations

GitHub is a hosting platform for software repositories using the git version control protocol, that also provides additional features such as wikis, issue-tracking, discussion boards. GitHub is an example of a social network where users can comment on commits, fork repositories, create branches, make pull requests etc.

We developed a multi-agent GitHub and Twitter simulations using DASH agents [4,11]. In our GitHub simulation model DASH communication hubs provide access to repositories and other shared state information. DASH agents perform action on repositories (e.g. push to a repository, make a pull request, etc.). Agents' decision process is based on past history of interactions with repositories which could is obtained from historical training data. If historical data on interactions is not available agents use generalized model to choose action and repository. Frequency of actions is obtained from historical training data as well.

In our Twitter simulation model DASH communication hubs provide access to popular tweets and conversation threads. DASH agents perform actions such as tweet, retweet, quote, reply, etc.

4.3   Experiment Setup

The following simplification operators were applied to the GitHub simulation:

Random Subsamples of User Agents. The following sample sizes were used: 0.1 M, 0.4 M, 0.8 M, 1 M, 1.2 M, 1.4 M, 1.8 M. One month of training data contains 1.9 M users.

Random subsamples of repositories. The following sample sizes were used: 0.1 M, 0.2 M, 0.4 M, 0.8 M, 1.6 M, 2.4 M. One month of training data contains 2.8 M repositories.

Random subsamples of training events. The following sample sizes were used: 10 K, 0.1 M, 1 M, 10 M, 20 M. The total number of events in the training data (1 month) was 31 M.

Different amount of training data − 1d, 2d, 4d, 1 week, 2 weeks, 1 month, 2 months of training intervals were used. This simplification picks a chronological window and keeps only the agents, repositories and events that appear in that window.

Simplifying agent's behavior by reducing the number of possible event types users can produce.

Random subsamples of training events and different event types combined together. This is simplification applies to operators: Random subsamples of training events (10 K, 0.1 M, 1 M, 10 M, 20 M events) and simplification of agents' behavior by reducing the number of possible event types users can produce (only half of the most frequent event types was used).

Frequency-based subsampling of user agents. Only agents with the highest rates of actions were selected. We used the following subsample sizes: 0.1 M, 0.4 M, 0.8 M, 1 M, 1.2 M

Frequency-based subsampling of user repositories. Only agents that interact with repositories that have highest rates of actions on them were selected. We used the following subsample sizes: 0.1 M, 0.2 M, 0.4 M, 0.8 M, 1.6 M

Push star agents is a simplification of agent actions. It was observed that some users tend to produce long sequences of action (in this case it was push to a repository) that are repeated over time. Push star agents instead of making each push individually produce batched of such actions, which should potentially reduce time on handling each action individually.

Agents aggregated into team/group agents. We ran experiments with 100 K, 400 K, 700 K users grouped into teams. Teams are defined as sub-clusters (sub-graphs) of users that interact with shared set of repositories. Team agent is a simplification that aggregates properties of all users of the team and interacts with repositories of this team.

The following simplification operators were applied to Twitter simulation:

Random subsamples of user agents. The following sample sizes were used: 10 K, 50 K, 0.1 M, 0.2 M, 0.4 M, 0.6 M. One month of training data contains 0.65 M users.

Random subsamples of tweets. The following sample sizes were used: 0.1 M, 0.2 M, 0.4 M, 0.8 M, 1.6 M. One month of training data contains 1.6 M events.

Random subsamples of training events (tweets, retweets, quotes, replies, etc.). The following sample sizes were used: 0.1 M, 0.2 M, 0.4 M, 0.8 M, 1.6 M.

Different amount of training data – 1d, 2d, 4d, 1 week, 2 weeks, 1 month, 2 months of training intervals were used.

Frequency-based subsampling of user agents. Only agents with the highest rates of actions were selected. We used the following subsample sizes: 0.1 M, 0.2 M, 0.3 M, 0.4 M, 0.6 M.

These simplifications are not mutually exclusive. In many instances they are applied together. We experimented with random subsamples of training events applied together with reducing the actions considered by each agent. Another example is the different amount of training operator, which can be applied together with any simplification operator.

One month of training data with all users and resources (repositories, tweets, etc.) is considered a full-scale simulation, although it is also just one possible value of the operator.

5 Results

To evaluate quality of predictions of our simulation models we used we use the following metrics for the GitHub simulation:

User popularity - top 5000 most popular users, popularity measured as the total number of *watch* and *fork* events on repositories owned by user. Calculated as Rank-Biased Overlap between ground truth and simulation (RBO) [16].

Community Contributing users - the proportion of users who interact with a community and who are active contributors, making commits and pull requests to community repositories. Calculated as absolute difference between ground truth and simulation.

User activity distribution - the distribution of the number of events produced by users. Calculated as Jensen-Shannon (JS) divergence [7].

For Twitter simulation we used the following metrics:

User activity distribution - the distribution of the number of events produced by users. Calculated as JS divergence (ground truth vs. simulation).

Most active users - the top 5000 users with the most events. Calculated as Rank-Biased Overlap between ground truth and simulation (RBO) [16].

Every point in each figure represents a simplification operator applied to the original simulation model. Each point corresponds to a specific configuration parameter of the operator. For example, subsample size is a configuration parameter of random user, repository, event subsampling operators; the number of supported events is a parameters of the reduction of event types generated by agent. Each point is an average of 7 runs, confidence intervals are plotted on both axes.

Ranges of operators' parameters were selected manually. Automated search may allow to find suboptimal settings with fine granularity for a given metric and resource (memory and runtime) constraints.

For all metrics higher is better, 1 is the best value (perfect prediction), 0 is the lowest possible value. Figures 1 a, b show GitHub simulation evaluation metrics, runtime and memory used. As a baseline for comparison we chose simulation that uses one month of training and instantiates all agents and uses all resources from training data. For GitHub it is 1.9 M users and 3.2 M repositories, baseline simulation consumes 24.5 Gb of memory and 26 min of runtime. For Twitter it is 650 K users and 1.6 M tweets, baseline simulation consumes 7.8 Gb of memory and 172 min of runtime.

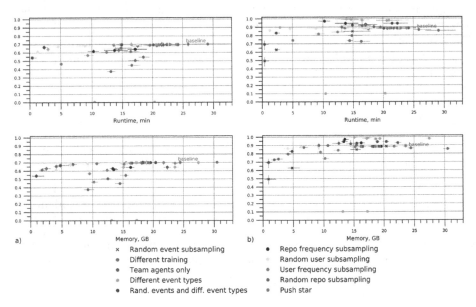

Fig. 1. GitHub: a) User popularity, b) Community contributing users

In Fig. 1a, the random event subsampling shows the same results as random user subsampling and performs better on most of the data points. The random event subsampling operator reduces simulation runtime by 48% compare to random user subsampling and different amount of training operators. Applying this operator allows almost twice as many iterations as the full-scale simulation with perfect performance, or six times as many with 97% of the original score.

In Fig. 1b reducing the types of actions that GitHub agents perform reduces noise and produces better scores than the full-scale simulation. Most subsampling operators converge on values close to 0.9 (10% difference between ground truth and simulation) where the reduced number of events operator shows values close to 0.98. At the same time it also reduces runtime and memory use in half compared to baseline.

Applying both random event subsampling and reducing the number of event types simultaneously improved performance on the community contributing users metric. This means that combining different operators can potentially produce better results than individual operators applied separately.

In the Twitter simulation both metrics (most active users - Fig. 2a, user activity distribution - Fig. 2b most of the simplification operators significantly reduce runtime and memory. For example, the frequency-based user subsampling that takes top 300 K users (about 50% of the whole data set) reduces runtime from 172 min to 43 min and memory from 7.8 Gb to 5.3 Gb. Random tweet subsampling reduces runtime to 20 min and memory use to 6 Gb on 100K tweet sample.

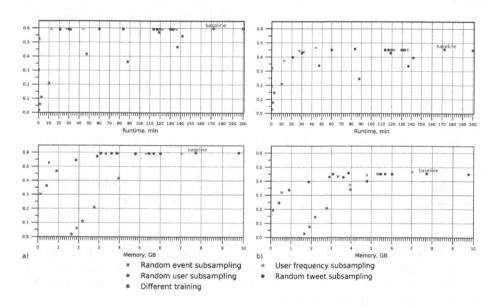

Fig. 2. Twitter: a) Most active users, b) User activity distribution

6 Semi-automated Search for Effective Simplifications

As can be seen from the previous section, some simplifications may have a dramatic effect on runtime and memory consumption for some metrics while maintaining high performance. However the best simplification is problem-dependent: random user subsampling predicts user popularity on GitHub very well in a small fraction of the time, for example, but performs poorly on both metrics for Twitter, where frequency-based subsampling shines. Removing the right subset of actions in GitHub can reduce errors in predicting community contributing users by over 90% while running in half the time.

Finding a set of simplifications, their configurations and combinations for a simulation model is an optimization problem where the objective function balances the quality of simulation results and resource usage. We propose a tool that partially automates this process and allows researchers to find simplification configurations that yield the best results within given resource constraints. Each simplification can be viewed as a parameterized operator that is applied to the original simulation. The developer may supply domain-dependent simplification operators that make use of domain features.

If an operator's parameter space has an ordering, it is possible to use gradient descent optimization algorithms to find optimal configurations for parameters, or to use various heuristics to traverse the parameter space in search of suboptimal solution. For example, a subsampling simplification can be used with binary search on the proportion of agents to keep. This approach complements analytic approaches of e.g. [6] since it is empirical, relying on observed performance of simplified simulations. Accretion and removal operators can be used to search for the optimal set of actions for a simplified agent to consider.

7   Conclusions and Future Work

Our experiments with simplifications show that it is possible to reduce computational complexity (memory and runtime) of the simulation and preserve accuracy of the simulation. Simplifications can use domain agnostic and domain dependent algorithms. They may target specific quality metrics and properties of the simulation model. Simplifications may be applied in combination with each other.

In our experiments we demonstrated several instances of simplifications with different quality metrics on simulation of two social networks - GitHub and Twitter. In several cases simplifications reduced runtime of Twitter simulation by 85% and memory by 32%. In GitHub simulations simplifying agents' behavior by reducing the number of supported actions/events reduced error in simulation predictions to the ground truth by 90%. These findings show that applying simplifications can be useful if computational resources are constrained and simulation models requires many runs.

Possible combinations of simplifications (possible parameter values) as well as their configurations create a parameter space. The process of finding simplification settings that fit resource constraints can also be automated. Our preliminary experiments with automated search for parameters under specified runtime and memory constraints show that it is feasible to automatically identify good configurations and simplification parameters. In the future work we will explore various strategies for simplifications and their parameters. We will also add the capability for our search tool to propose and apply combinations of simplification operators dynamically.

Acknowledgements. The authors thank the Defense Advanced Research Projects Agency (DARPA), contract W911NF-17-C-0094, for their support.

References

1. Blythe, J., Tregubov, A.: FARM: architecture for distributed agent-based social simulations. In: Lin, D., Ishida, T., Zambonelli, F., Noda, I. (eds.) MMAS 2018. LNCS (LNAI), vol. 11422, pp. 96–107. Springer, Cham (2019). https://doi.org/10. 1007/978-3-030-20937-7_7
2. Blythe, J., et al.: The darpa socialsim challenge: massive multi-agent simulations of the github ecosystem. In: Proceedings of AAMAS, pp. 1835–1837 (2019)
3. Blythe, J., et al.: Massive multi-agent data-driven simulations of the github ecosystem. In: Demazeau, Y., Matson, E., Corchado, J.M., De la Prieta, F. (eds.) PAAMS 2019. LNCS (LNAI), vol. 11523, pp. 3–15. Springer, Cham (2019). https://doi.org/ 10.1007/978-3-030-24209-1_1
4. Blythe, J., Tregubov, A.: DASH website (2020). https://dash-agents.github.io/
5. Cohen, M., Dam, M., Lomuscio, A., Russo, F.: Abstraction in model checking multi-agent systems. In: Proceedings of AAMAS, pp. 945–952 (2009)
6. Kleer, J.: Dynamic domain abstraction through meta-diagnosis. In: Miguel, I., Ruml, W. (eds.) SARA 2007. LNCS (LNAI), vol. 4612, pp. 109–123. Springer, Heidelberg (2007). https://doi.org/10.1007/978-3-540-73580-9_11
7. DeDeo, S., Hawkins, R., Klingenstein, S., Hitchcock, T.: Bootstrap methods for the empirical study of decision-making and information flows in social systems. Entropy **15**(12), 2246–2276 (2013). https://doi.org/10.3390/e15062246
8. Edmonds, B., Moss, S.: From KISS to KIDS – An *'Anti-simplistic' Modelling Approach.* In: Davidsson, P., Logan, B., Takadama, K. (eds.) MABS 2004. LNCS (LNAI), vol. 3415, pp. 130–144. Springer, Heidelberg (2005). https://doi.org/10. 1007/978-3-540-32243-6_11
9. Giunchiglia, F., Walsh, T.: A theory of abstraction. Artif. Intell. **57**(2–3), 323–389 (1992)
10. Knoblock, C.A.: Automatically generating abstractions for planning. Artif. Intell. **68**(2), 243–302 (1994)
11. Murić, G., et al.: The darpa socialsim challenge: cross-platform multi-agent simulations. In: Proceedings of the 19th International Conference on Autonomous Agents and MultiAgent Systems. AAMAS 2020 (2020)
12. Onggo, B.S., Karpat, O.: Agent-based conceptual model representation using BPMN. In: Proceedings of the Winter Simulation Conference, pp. 671–682 (2011)
13. Rhodes, D.M., Holcombe, M., Qwarnstrom, E.E.: Reducing complexity in an agent based reaction model-benefits and limitations of simplifications in relation to run time and system level output. Biosystems **147**, 21–27 (2016)
14. Shirazi, A.S., Davison, T., von Mammen, S., Denzinger, J., Jacob, C.: Adaptive agent abstractions to speed up spatial agent-based simulations. Simul. Model. Pract. Theor. **40**, 144–160 (2014)
15. Struss, P.: A theory of model simplification and abstraction for diagnosis. In: Proceedings of 5th International Workshop on Qualitative Reasoning, pp. 25–57 (1991)
16. Webber, W., Moffat, A., Zobel, J.: A similarity measure for indefinite rankings. ACM Trans. Inf. Syst. **28**(4), 1–38 (2010)

Improved Travel Demand Modeling with Synthetic Populations

Kaidi Wang[1]([✉]) [iD], Wenwen Zhang[1] [iD], Henning Mortveit[2,3] [iD],
and Samarth Swarup[3]

[1] Urban Affairs and Planning, Virginia Tech,
Blacksburg, VA 24061, USA
{kaidi,wenwenz3}@vt.edu
[2] Department of Engineering Systems and Environment, University of Virginia,
Charlottesville, VA 22911, USA
henning.mortveit@virginia.edu
[3] Biocomplexity Institute and Initiative, University of Virginia,
Charlottesville, VA 22911, USA
swarup@virginia.edu

Abstract. We compare synthetic population-based travel demand modeling with the state of the art travel demand models used by metropolitan planning offices in the United States. Our comparison of the models for three US cities shows that synthetic population-based models match the state of the art models closely for the temporal trip distributions and the spatial distribution of destinations. The advantages of the synthetic population-based method are that it provides greater spatial resolution, can be generalized to any region, and can be used for studying correlations with demographics and activity types, which are useful for modeling the effects of policy changes.

Keywords: Travel demand · Transportation · Synthetic population

1 Introduction

Travel demand modeling refers to modeling population movements within a region, typically over the course of a fixed time period such as day or a week. Mobility depends on a number of factors, such as demographics, transportation infrastructure, the build environment, and more.

Transportation planning and demand modeling are required to receive federal transportation funds for larger urban areas in the U.S. [9]. Based the most recent regulation, the Safe, Accountable, Flexible, Efficient Transportation Equity Act: A Legacy for Users (SAFETEA-LU), transportation plans need to address many requirements, such as air quality issues, multimodal planning, better manage the existing system, expand public input, and financial requirements [15]. Transportation demand models play very important roles in forecasting and assessing whether the proposed transportation planning alternatives can help the region

© Springer Nature Switzerland AG 2021
S. Swarup and B. T. R. Savarimuthu (Eds.): MABS 2020, LNAI 12316, pp. 94–105, 2021.
https://doi.org/10.1007/978-3-030-66888-4_8

to meet the corresponding requirements. Therefore, all Metropolitan Planning Organizations (MPOs) for areas with population more than 50,000 have to develop, implement, and calibrate local travel demand models to evaluate a broad range of alternatives [9].

This has some limitations. First, MPOs don't do this planning for smaller regions. Thus, the coverage doesn't extend over the whole country. Second, there is a lack of spatial refinement in existing models, as all trips are attributed to Traffic Analysis Zones (TAZs), as we explain in the next section. Third, these models are not applicable in abnormal situations, such as mobility during disasters.

To address these limitations, we are exploring the use of synthetic populations [2,20], which provide a disaggregated model of the population, their activity schedules, and activity locations. The synthetic population approach to generating travel demand is described in Sect. 3.

In the present work, we compare the synthetic population-derived travel demand with the travel demand generated by two models used by MPOs, for three US cities. The goals are to see how closely the models match, what the differences are, and where the synthetic population approach might be improved. Once the approach is validated, we can use it to do travel demand modeling for all regions in the US.

2   State of the Art in Mobility Modeling

Currently, a majority of MPOs in the United States adopt two genres of travel demand models, namely the conventional four-step travel demand model and the latest activity-based travel model. The four-step model is a widely adopted transportation demand forecast framework that can be dated back to the 1950s [19]. The model adopts four specific steps, including trip generation, trip distribution, mode choice, and trip assignment, to forecast future travel demand given changes in the spatial distribution in employment and population and performance of a transportation system within a region. The first trip generation step estimates the number of produced and attracted trips for each Traffic Analysis Zone (TAZ). The trip distribution step connects trip origins to destinations, which results in a person trip Origin-Destination (OD) matrix. The mode choice step divides the person trip OD matrix by travel mode, such as passenger vehicles, transit, etc., and generates mode-specific OD matrices for vehicle trips by the time of the day. The last trip assignment component forecasts the route for trips. The unit of analysis for the four-step model is zone-level trips. Thus, the model is not sensitive to demand and supply policies, as individual decision making is barely incorporated in the model [9].

The activity-based model advances the four-step model by forecasting travel demand at a more refined unit of analysis [5]. The activity-based model is typically developed at a disaggregated person level, enabling the model to evaluate possible changes in travel behavior and system performances across policy scenarios. However, the modeled geographic unit is similar to the four-step model, which is typically TAZs. In other words, all activities, trip origins, and destinations are assigned to TAZ centroids. Some MPOs tend to adopt more refined TAZ boundaries in the activity-based model compared with the four-step model [4]. The activity-based models, however, are more data and computational resource-consuming compared with the four-step model. Thus, only a limited number of MPOs have adopted the activity-based model [10]. Though several MPOs have started to migrate from the four-step model to the activity-based model, the four-step model remains the most commonly used travel demand model in the U.S [10].

Both of the aforementioned demand forecasting frameworks were developed for regional planning purposes. In those scenarios, a TAZ-level model is considered sufficient for planning-related decision making. However, the model fails to support policy making at refined spatial scales to address emerging transportation problems (e.g., chaotic curb uses) introduced by disruptive transportation modes, especially ride-hailing services and the envisioned Shared and Private Autonomous Vehicles (AVs). Even after incorporating these emerging travel modes into the four-step [28] and activity models [12,30], the model outputs are constrained at TAZ level, which are not very useful to support refined decision making, such as block level curb spaces allocation. Meanwhile, the ride-hailing companies, such as Uber and Lyft, are reluctant to release detailed trip data, due to competition and privacy concerns. Finally, different MPOs tend to model mobility demand using various data sources (e.g., National Household Travel Survey [NHTS] vs. local household travel survey) and are calibrated using different base year data, rendering it difficulty to conduct research for cross-city and region comparisons [19].

Therefore, in this study, we proposed a disaggregated travel demand modeling approach that is built upon synthetic populations (developed using multiple datasets, as described in the next section) and nationally available transportation network and Point of Interest (PoI) data to fill the current demand model and data gaps. We validate our modeling outputs by comparing spatiotemporal distributions of synthesized trips with Origin-Destination (OD) matrices (i.e., the product of mode choice). The OD matrices contain the number of estimated trips for each pair of origin and destination. Given that in most regions, vehicle travel is the dominant travel mode, our comparison will only focus on vehicle trips. We obtained OD matrices from three different regions with various urban forms, travel patterns and current transportation infrastructures, namely Richmond, VA, Seattle, WA, and Atlanta, GA. The adopted travel demand models differ across these cities, in terms of travel demand data sources, modeling framework, and modelled time periods, as displayed in Table 1.

Table 1. Model settings for validation OD metrics

Model settings	Atlanta, GA	Richmond, VA	Seattle, WA
Model framework	Activity-based	Four-step	Four-step
Model data source	2011 local survey	2009 NHTS	2014–2015 local survey
Calibrated base year	2015	2012	2014
Model time periods	5	4	12

3   The Synthetic Population Approach

A "synthetic population" [2,11,16] is a very detailed model of a region, including the resident population, their daily or weekly activity patterns, their networks of interaction, and the built environment. The last includes buildings, and also infrastructures for transportation, power, communication, etc. The synthetic populations have been used as the basis for multi-agent simulations in a variety of domains, including computational epidemiology [14], disaster response [6], transportation planning [3,30], and more [24,27]. They provide high resolution, high fidelity representations, enabling realistic simulations which can be used for meaningful policy recommendations [7]. A synthetic population is generated through a series of steps. We describe the initial steps briefly below, and present the mobility modeling step (assigning locations to activities) in more details. Further information is given in a technical report [20].

Generating Agents with Demographics: We use data from the American Community Survey [25], which provides demographic distributions for each blockgroup and a 5% sample of complete records for a slightly larger area, known as the Public Use Microdata Sample (PUMS). These are combined using the statistical technique called Iterative Proportional Fitting (IPF) [8,13] to generate a joint distribution over selected demographic variables. We chose *age of householder*, *household income*, and *household size* as the variables for the IPF step. From this, we sample the resulting joint distribution and select matching households from the PUMS data to create the population of synthetic agents.

Assigning Activity Patterns: Each person p created in the previous step is assigned an *activity sequence* $\alpha(p) = (a_{i,p})_i$ where each *activity* $a_{i,p}$ has a start time, a duration, and an activity type. For the synthetic population used in this work, the activity types are from the set

$$\mathcal{A} = \{\mathtt{Home}, \mathtt{Work}, \mathtt{School}, \mathtt{Shopping}, \mathtt{Religion}, \mathtt{Other}\}. \tag{1}$$

The activity sequence survey data was taken from the National Household Travel Survey (NHTS) 2017 [23]. From this, consistent week-long activity sequences were constructed and assigned using CART and the Fitted Values Means method [18].

Assigning Locations to Activities: This modeling step connects people and their activities to the set $\mathcal{L}$ of *residence-* and *activity locations* of the given region.

The first part of this modeling step constructs the *locations*. This is done based on the MS Building Footprint data [21] which we have augmented with a residential/non-residential classification based on the HERE Premium StreetMap landuse classifications and extended POI listings [17]. Each non-residence location, which we refer to as an *activity location*, is additionally augmented with a weight for each non-Home activity reflecting the likelihood of people conducting that particular activity at the given location. Each household is mapped to a residence location. The assignment of residence locations is done for each blockgroup. First each possible residence location is assigned one household, to ensure that there are no residence locations without at least one household. The remaining households are assigned residence locations with probability proportional to the area of the building footprint.

The second step assigns people's activities to locations. Abstractly, for each person p this step constructs a map $\lambda_p : \alpha(p) \longrightarrow \mathcal{L}$ that assigns to each activity $a_{i,p}$ of p a location $\ell \in \mathcal{L}$. For the various activity types, this algorithm has the following sequence of steps:

- Using NCES data [22], assign to each residence, the vector-valued ID containing the nearest public school for each grade level;
- Construct the normalized county/county work commute flow matrix M adjusted with county self-references using ACS commute flow data [1];
- For each person p:
  - assign each activity a_i of type Home to the residence location of p;
  - assign each activity a_i of type School to the age-appropriate school location assigned to their residence location;
  - select a work location using this 2-step process: (a) randomly select a target county c' using the probability distribution M_c where c is the county of p. (b) For county c', randomly select a work location ℓ from the set of activity locations $\mathcal{L}_A|_{c'}$ of c' using the probability distribution induced by the locations' Work weights. Assign all Work activities of p to ℓ. Thus, each working person has a consistent work location for the entire period.
  - if c' supports Shopping (resp. Other), assign Shopping (resp. Other) activities independently at random to the set of activity locations $\mathcal{L}_A|_{c'}$ of c' using the distribution induced by their Shopping (resp. Other) weights. If c' has no activity locations supporting Shopping (resp. Other), repeat this process using the home county c. If c does not support Shopping (resp. Other), select a county using the probability distribution M_c and repeat.
  - if c supports Religion, randomly select a location ℓ from the set of activity locations $\mathcal{L}_A|_c$ of c using the distribution induced by their Religion weights. If c has no activity location supporting Religion, select a county c'' using the probability distribution M_c and repeat for c''.

- Additionally, one may construct a person-person contact network using some form of location co-occupancy model; we do not need that for this work.

In the present work, we extract the collection of activities that take place on a Tuesday. Travel demand is constructed from the activity schedules by extracting the locations for successive activities. The start time for the travel is taken to be the end time of the first activity. If two successive activities take place at the same location, there is no travel, and this pair is not included in the travel demand file. Next we describe the comparison between travel demand constructed from synthetic populations and travel demand data obtained from three US MPOs, who use traditional models.

4   Comparison of Results

We validated the synthetic approach by comparing the distributions of synthesized trips with that of OD matrices generated by local travel demand models, using data from three cities, namely Richmond, VA, Atlanta, GA, and Seattle, WA. These three cities are selected because they tend to have significantly different urban forms and transit infrastructures. Cities like Richmond and Atlanta have more urban sprawl and have limited transit systems, while Seattle is more densely developed and maintains an extensive transit system. Specifically, we compared the number of generated trips, the distributions of trip departure times, as well as the spatial distributions of the trip origins and destinations, to determine if the synthetic trips are representative and can replicate the distributions generated by travel demand models, including both the activity-based model and the conventional four-step model.

4.1   Trip Counts Comparison

The number of trips generated by each approach for each city is illustrated in Table 2. For the three study areas, we only compare the trips that both start and end within the city boundaries. The number of daily trips generated by four-step travel demand model in Richmond is 370,998. Synthetic approach generates 401,042 daily trips, which is 8.1% more than that in four-step travel demand model. Seattle also sees slightly more synthetic trips. Notice that the Richmond travel demand model is calibrated using 2012 ACS data, while the Seattle model is calibrated using 2014 ACS data. The accuracy of the projected 2017 OD matrices from these models may vary depending on the quality of local population and employment forecasting model. The synthetic trips are generated using 2017 ACS data, which should be considered as more accurate compared with local forecasts. It is interesting that Atlanta's activity model generates significantly more trips than synthetic trips. ARC calibrated and validated the activity-based model (ABM) using 2011 regional household travel survey and then forecast travel demand in 2015, while the synthetic trip profiles are generated using 2017 NHTS data. This is largely because the synthetic population method assigns some destinations to locations outside the Census blockgroups that are within the city of Atlanta. These get eliminated when we restrict our analysis to travel demand in Atlanta. There may be two additional reasons for the discrepancy in daily trip generation: (1) the trip generation rate for Atlanta may decrease from 2011 to 2017, and (2) Atlanta NHTS data are not representative in the 2017 survey. In the concluding section, we address the possibility of reducing this discrepancy by using other data sets. It is important to note that the synthetic population model is generated for the entire state, so the total number of trips taken by the residents of Atlanta are not fully represented here. In other words, the discrepancy is not due to a systematic bias in the travel demand, but due to the fact that we are restricting the analysis to a subregion.

Table 2. Trip counts comparison

City	# of trips obtained from MPO	# of synthetic trips	Percentage difference
Richmond	370,998	401,042	8.1%
Seattle	1,087,814	1,152,136	5.6%
Atlanta	1,087,418	796,688	−26.7%

4.2 Departure Time Comparison

The number and percentage of trips by the periods of departure time is shown in Table 3 for each city. Overall, the temporal patterns of trips generated by the travel demand model and synthetic approach are similar. The share of trips in each of the time periods by the two methods is close. Thus, we conclude that the distribution of departure time of synthetic trips matches that in demand models. Notice that Seattle and Atlanta have more time periods in their travel demand model. We aggregated the trips into 4 time periods to make the comparison more intuitive. The MPO for Richmond defined AM period as 6:30 am–8:30 am and PM period as 4:30 pm–6:30 pm. ARC has five periods in the ABM. i.e. early morning, morning, midday, afternoon, evening. We collapsed early morning and evening into a night period. Finally, the AM period is 6 am–10 am and PM period is 3 pm–7 pm. Puget Sound Regional Council (PSRC), the MPO for Seattle, used 12 periods in the demand model. We aligned the periods with the other two cities as much as possible and end up with AM period between 7 am–10 am and PM period between 4 pm–8 pm. The synthetic population model gives actual trip start times, so it can be aggregated for any definition of the bins. In any case, the definition of time periods does not influence the comparison of models as we compare for each period rather than across periods.

Table 3. Trip count by time period

Period	Model	Richmond	Seattle	Atlanta
AM	Synthetic	54,996 (14%)	251,371 (22%)	190,226 (24%)
	Demand model	34,563 (9%)	191,111 (18%)	216,115 (20%)
MD	Synthetic	201,063 (50%)	453,975 (39%)	258,049 (32%)
	Demand model	198,413 (53%)	402,391 (37%)	399,421 (37%)
PM	Synthetic	68,554 (17%)	316,430 (27%)	258,057 (32%)
	Demand model	42,648 (11%)	371,374 (34%)	305,209 (28%)
NT	Synthetic	76,429 (19%)	130,360 (11%)	90,356 (11%)
	Demand model	95,374 (26%)	122,938 (11%)	166,673 (15%)

4.3 Spatial Distribution Comparison

We validated the spatial distributions of the trips by examining the spatial correlation of buffered trip origins and destinations. Each origin or destination is a traffic analysis zone (TAZ). There are 219 TAZs in Richmond, 856 TAZs in Seattle and 829 TAZs in Atlanta. Table 4 shows the computed correlations using data from two sources by time periods for each city. A buffered TAZ includes a TAZ and its neighbor TAZs based on queen contiguity criteria, which means if two TAZs share a vertex or edge, they are neighbors. The reason we do not directly impute spatial correlation of origins and destinations is that the correlation cannot reflect the actual spatial pattern. For example, the spatial correlation of destinations could be extremely low even though the synthetic trips end in areas close to the destinations of trips in demand model. Including neighbor TAZs when comparing the distribution will mitigate this issue.

Table 4. Spatial distribution pearson correlation of origins and destinations

City	AM	MD	PM	NT
Correlations of origins				
Richmond	0.85	0.79	0.73	0.81
Seattle	0.86	0.53	0.40	0.54
Atlanta	0.84	0.71	0.65	0.82
Correlations of destinations				
Richmond	0.62	0.77	0.85	0.83
Seattle	0.35	0.58	0.70	0.39
Atlanta	0.58	0.73	0.84	0.86

It can be observed that the spatial correlation of origins peaks in AM and that of destinations peaks in PM or NT for all of the three cities. In contrast, they all experience least correlated origins in PM and destinations in AM. The low correlation is because of different methods of estimating employment in the two approaches. MPOs estimate employment based on ACS block-level data while the synthetic approach uses county-level commute flows. The destinations in AM and origins in PM are mostly the locations of jobs. Therefore, the different estimates lead to low correlations. This indicates one aspect in which the synthetic population model can be refined.

As shown in Table 4, the destinations in AM in Seattle is the least spatially correlated in all the cities and periods. Their spatial distribution is illustrated in Fig. 1. Both maps demonstrate that the trips tend to end in commercial zones such as downtown Seattle in the middle, industrial district in the southeast and Northgate in the north. Only a small portion of trips travel to Northeast Seattle and Ballard, where most land use type is residential zones. Notice that the very west and very east areas in the map are mostly water areas. Therefore, few trips end there. In general, the spatial distribution of synthetic trips matches that of trips generated by the MPOs well.

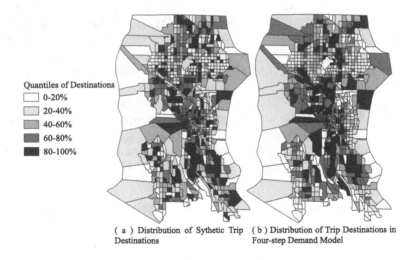

(a) Distribution of Sythetic Trip   (b) Distribution of Trip Destinations in
Destinations   Four-step Demand Model

Fig. 1. Distribution of destinations in AM in Seattle

5   Conclusion

This study evaluated the synthetic population-based model by comparing it with the state of the art travel demand models used by Metropolitan Planning Offices in the United States. This was done by comparing the spatial and temporal distribution of the trips generated by the two approaches. The results indicate that the trip count estimated by synthetic approach is close to that estimated by travel demand model. The synthetic approach matches demand models for the distribution of departure times. The spatial correlations of origins and destinations are mostly high except some specific periods. The low spatial correlation of origins in PM and destinations in AM reflects the difference of the two models. The synthetic population model uses ACS county-county commuter flows, but within counties chooses destinations randomly (though weighted by an estimate of building capacity). Switching to a higher resolution, such as the Census LODES data product [26], might help with this.

Synthetic population-based models are more flexible compared to four-step travel demand model. They are less computationally expensive compared to activity-based model while providing more details on the trips and the travelers. Besides, this approach is generalizable that most areas can use it to estimate travel demand. Thus it can be used to do a multiple city study as it enables direct comparison between cities. Future work can also be to combine it with research on automated vehicles. For example, the social interaction potential could be explored with a shared automated vehicle (SAV) system using synthetic trips as input, e.g., by integrating with simulations of potential shared autonomous vehicle use [28, 29].

Acknowledgments. We thank our external collaborators and members of the Network Systems Science and Advanced Computing (NSSAC) division for their suggestions and comments. This work was partially supported by DTRA Grant HDTRA1-17-F-0118 and NASA grant 80NSSC18K1594. We also thank Atlanta Regional Commission (ARC), Puget Sound Regional Council (PSRC) and Richmond Regional Planning District Commission for providing us with travel demand model outputs.

Any opinions, findings, and conclusions or recommendations expressed in this material are those of the authors and do not necessarily reflect the views, official policies or endorsements, either expressed or implied, of NASA, DTRA, or the U.S. Government.

References

1. 2011-2015 5-year ACS commuting flows. https://www.census.gov/data/tables/2015/demo/metro-micro/commuting-flows-2015.html. Accessed 24 Feb 2020
2. Adiga, A., et al.: Generating a synthetic population of the United States. Technical report, NDSSL 15–009, Network Dynamics and Simulation Science Laboratory, Virginia Bioinformatics Institute, Virginia Tech (2015)
3. Adiga, A., Marathe, M., Mortveit, H., Wu, S., Swarup, S.: Modeling urban transportation in the aftermath of a nuclear disaster: the role of human behavioral responses. In: The Conference on Agent-Based Modeling in Transportation Planning and Operations, Blacksburg, VA, 30 September –2 October 2013 (2013)
4. Atlanta Regional Commission, et al.: Activity-based travel model specifications: coordinated travel-regional activity based modeling platform (CT-RAMP) for the Atlanta region (2012). http://documents.atlantaregional.com/The-Atlanta-Region-s-Plan/RTP/abm-specification-report.pdf
5. Axhausen, K.W., Gärling, T.: Activity-based approaches to travel analysis: conceptual frameworks, models, and research problems. Transp. Rev. **12**(4), 323–341 (1992)
6. Barrett, C., et al.: Planning and response in the aftermath of a large crisis: an agent-based informatics framework. In: Pasupathy, R., Kim, S.H., Tolk, A., Hill, R., Kuhl, M.E. (eds.) Proceedings of the 2013 Winter Simulation Conference, pp. 1515–1526. IEEE Press, Piscataway (2013)

7. Barrett, C., Eubank, S., Marathe, A., Marathe, M., Pan, Z., Swarup, S.: Information integration to support model-based policy informatics. Innov. J. **16**(1) (2011). Article 2
8. Beckman, R.J., Baggerly, K.A., McKay, M.D.: Creating synthetic base-line populations. Transp. Res. A Policy Pract. **30**, 415–429 (1996)
9. Beimborn, E., et al.: A transportation modeling primer (2006)
10. Castiglione, J., Bradley, M., Gliebe, J.: Activity-based travel demand models: a primer. No. SHRP 2 report S2–C46-RR-1 (2015)
11. Chapuis, K., Taillandier, P., Renaud, M., Drogoul, A.: Gen*: a generic toolkit to generate spatially explicit synthetic populations. Int. J. Geogr. Inf. Sci. **32**(6), 1194–1210 (2018)
12. Childress, S., Nichols, B., Charlton, B., Coe, S.: Using an activity-based model to explore the potential impacts of automated vehicles. Transp. Res. Rec. **2493**(1), 99–106 (2015)
13. Deming, W.E., Stephan, F.F.: On a least squares adjustment of a sampled frequency table when the expected marginal tables are known. Ann. Math. Stat. **11**(4), 427–444 (1940)
14. Eubank, S., et al.: Modelling disease outbreaks in realistic urban social networks. Nature **429**, 180–184 (2004)
15. Fischer, J.W., Resources, S., Division, I.: Safe, accountable, flexible, efficient transportation equity act-a legacy for users (SAFETEA-LU or SAFETEA): selected major provisions. Congressional Research Service, The Library of Congress (2005)
16. Gallagher, S., Richardson, L.F., Ventura, S.L., Eddy, W.F.: SPEW: synthetic populations and ecosystems of the world. J. Comput. Graph. Stat. **27**(4), 773–784 (2018)
17. HERE premium streetmap for the U.S. https://www.here.com/. Accessed 24 Feb 2020
18. Lum, K., Chungbaek, Y., Eubank, S., Marathe, M.: A two-stage, fitted values approach to activity matching. Int. J. Transp. **4**, 41–56 (2016). https://doi.org/10.14257/ijt.2016.4.1.03
19. McNally, M.G.: The four step model. In: Handbook of Transport Modelling, vol. 1, pp. 35–41 (2000)
20. Mortveit, H.S., et al.: Synthetic populations and interaction networks for the U.S. nSSAC Technical report #2019-025 (2020)
21. Microsoft building footprint data U.S. https://github.com/microsoft/USBuildingFootprints. Accessed 24 Feb 2020
22. National center for education statistics. https://nces.ed.gov/datatools/. Accessed 24 Feb 2020
23. National household travel survey. https://nhts.ornl.gov/. Accessed 24 Feb 2020
24. Swarup, S., Gohlke, J.M., Bohland, J.R.: A microsimulation model of population heat exposure. In: Proceedings of the 2nd International Workshop on Agent-Based Modeling of Urban Systems (ABMUS), São Paulo, Brazil (2017)
25. United States Census Bureau: American community survey 2013–2017 5-year estimates, American FactFinder. https://factfinder.census.gov/
26. U.S. Census Bureau: LEHD origin-destination employment statistics (LODES). https://lehd.ces.census.gov/data/
27. Waddell, P.: UrbanSim: modeling urban development for land use, transportation, and environmental planning. J. Am. Plann. Assoc. **68**(3), 297–314 (2002)
28. Zhang, W., Guhathakurta, S.: Parking spaces in the age of shared autonomous vehicles: how much parking will we need and where? Transp. Res. Rec. **2651**(1), 80–91 (2017)

29. Zhang, W., Guhathakurta, S., Fang, J., Zhang, G.: Exploring the impact of shared autonomous vehicles on urban parking demand: an agent-based simulation approach. Sustain. Cities Soc. **19**, 34–45 (2015)
30. Zhang, W., Mortveit, H.S., Swarup, S.: Estimating shared autonomous vehicle fleet size to meet urban daily travel demand. In: The 3rd International Workshop on Agent-Based Modeling of Urban Systems (ABMUS), Stockholm, Sweden (2018)

Author Index

Afshar Sedigh, Amir Hosein   66

Barthelemy, Johan   28
Blythe, Jim   81
Bogaerts, Toon   1
Bosmans, Stig   1

Casteels, Wim   1
Cheng, Hao   13

Denil, Joachim   1
Doshi-Velez, Finale   54

Frantz, Christopher K.   66

Hellinckx, Peter   1

Izumi, Kiyoshi   41

Johora, Fatema T.   13

Mercelis, Siegfried   1
Mortveit, Henning   94
Müller, Jörg P.   13

Nishimura, Yasutaka   41

Ou, Han Ching   54

Perez, Pascal   28
Purvis, Martin K.   66
Purvis, Maryam A.   66

Qian, Yan   28

Savarimuthu, Bastin Tony Roy   66
Sester, Monika   13
Shimura, Taichi   41
Swarup, Samarth   94

Tambe, Milind   54
Tregubov, Alexey   81

Wang, Kai   54
Wang, Kaidi   94

Yoshihara, Kiyohito   41

Zhang, Wenwen   94

Printed in the United States
By Bookmasters